BIG ISLAND OF HAWAII RESTAURANTS AND DINING

WITH HILO AND THE KONA COAST

INTIMATE BISTROS · CULINARY ADVENTURES · BEACH BARS
FINE DINING · WATERFRONT RESTAURANTS · LOCAL DIVES
COFFEE SHOPS · ROMANTIC HIDEAWAYS · BUDGET FINDS
CASUAL SPOTS · HOLE-IN-THE-WALLS · ETHNIC EATERIES

**HAWAII RESTAURANT GUIDE SERIES
ROBERT & CINDY CARPENTER**

REVISED EDITION

BIG ISLAND OF HAWAII
RESTAURANTS AND DINING
WITH HILO AND THE KONA COAST

1st Edition, Revised

ISBN-10 1-931752-40-0

ISBN-13 978-1-931752-40-4

Library of Congress Control Number: 2006910110

Printed in the United States of America

Holiday Publishing Inc.
Post Office Box 11120
Lahaina, HI 96761

holidaypublishing@yahoo.com

www.hawaiirestaurantguide.com

BIG ISLAND OF HAWAII
RESTAURANTS AND DINING
WITH HILO AND THE KONA COAST

TABLE OF CONTENTS

Introduction

Pundits say that there are those who eat to live and those that live to eat. Since you're reading this you probably already have a leaning toward the latter group. Well, join the club! Food has taken on an importance never seen before. That's not to say that Mom's cooking wasn't good. What better place can you think of to develop your own sense for comfort food than at the kitchen table? However, with restaurants popping up on every corner and 24 hours of food shows airing daily, culinary pursuits have definitely come of age.

Hawaii is the perfect place to explore this newfound enthusiasm. In the islands you'll find people from around the world blending and sharing the best of their cultures. Naturally the local dining scene reflects this international view where noodle shops and Continental dining venues make perfect neighbors. Then, just to make things more interesting Hawaii people like to include some neo-fusion cuisine and contemporary sushi to complete the neighborhood mix.

This book was written in an attempt to define this wonderful disarray. Knowing full well that this was a nigh on impossible task we took off happily into the fog and aren't quite sure if we've emerged yet! Let's just say that six islands, seven years and 1500 dissimilar restaurants, ethnic eateries and hole-in-the-walls later you now have in your hands a copy of Big Island Restaurants and Dining.

Along the path of creation we found ourselves continually testing the envelope. Before putting pen to paper there first came research, which of course was our favorite part of the undertaking! Being self-confessed culinary vagabonds what better way to combine vices than by taking a dining junket across the Hawaiian Islands? As the adventure continued it started taking on a Keseyian spin. When the term "fusion confusion" entered our daily vocabulary we knew the time had arrived to develop a master criterion. Here's what we determined:

Experience has taught us that adventurous travelers like to be empowered. They don't care for travel experiences that include being shoved on a bus and handed a meal voucher. Nor do they like to be led around to all the standard guidebook hot spots. No, they want to go it alone and make their own decisions whenever possible. It became our goal to provide the support material required to do so.

To begin with people need to have accurate information concerning the physical location, website address, phone number, hours of operation, dress code, style of cuisine, credit cards and price range of each establishment. Then they like to see actual menu items with prices to determine budgeting. What might be a medium priced place to one person could be something entirely different to another!

Our restaurant selection process follows suit. We decided early on not to waste time writing about places we wouldn't bother revisiting and skipped right over to creating an A list. Why waste time beating up on also-rans when there are so many wonderful places to talk about? The results have been assembled into a collection that covers a range of tastes and styles from elegant to elemental.

Of course no restaurant guide would be complete without impressions. People have repeatedly told us that they want to know what to expect before they arrive. This can run the gamut from finding a parking place to personal preferences like waterfront dining. In our comment sections we try to deal with real world issues and leave the chamber of commerce spin to the paid inclusion publishers.

Finally, all of this was done at our own expense. Too much of what vacationers encounter is biased by compensation. In the realm of travel payola is offered in many forms. It could be through a free cruise, complimentary meals or outright cash payment. Regardless, the resulting work becomes an advertorial instead of an honest review. It's hard to be objective when they roll out the red carpet!

This brings us to the bane of all restaurant writers - timeliness. The travel world is constantly changing and no part changes faster than menus. Restaurateurs all seem to have revolving doors on their operations! So was creating this work an act of futility? We think not. Looking back over the last decade we see far more continuity than interruption.

It's our hope that you will enjoy this guide as a travelogue rather than consign it to the dusty reference shelf. Think of it as a personal journal and it will take you far. Life isn't perfect and neither is this book. Sure, a certain dish you spotted in a review may no longer be offered, but ask about the new special on the current menu and stretch your horizons. Isn't that why you came here in the first place?

And what if a stop turns out to be a complete catastrophe? Do what we do and laugh! When the host greets us with, "Hope you're not trying to catch a plane." Our standard response is, "Welcome to the islands!" Even the best restaurants have off-days. Chefs go on vacations like everyone else so maintain a positive attitude and major inconveniences will later seem like minor footnotes.

Enjoy your visit to Hawaii's Big Island. Explore the renowned sights and sounds found in the islands. But during your travels be sure to set time aside to discover the culturally diverse culinary experiences unique to America's Pacific Paradise!

Robert & Cindy Carpenter
Authors

Old Haunts

People ask us all sorts of questions, but "Is the local drive-in still open?" ranks near the top. This comes as no surprise as the restaurant business is well-known for its low margins and high mortality. Like everywhere else restaurants on The Big Island come and go. A tourism based economy might sound like a ticket to prosperity, but consider the challenges posed by scale and distance. Combine a small market with 2500 miles of ocean and everything involved gets pricey.

We've decided to start this work by acknowledging some old favorites that have stepped to the sidelines. If your travels brought you to The Big Island during the last decade you may recognize a name or two. Otherwise, understand that many good times were had by those fortunate enough to remember these places:

Bianelli's	Kailua-Kona
Edelweiss	Waimea
Edwards at Kanaloa	Keauhou
Kona Ranch House	Kailua-Kona
Maha's Café	Waimea
Parker Ranch Grill	Waimea
Restaurant Kaikodo	Hilo
Sam Choy's Kaloko	Kailua-Kona
Sibu Café	Kailua-Kona
Surt's	Volcano Village

That brings us to the next group of suspects. Long time Big Island people should remember the island before mill closings and lava flows changed its face. Those were years of colorful entrepreneurs and restaurants whose time has now passed. See if any of the following strikes a chord in your memory banks:

Dorian's	Kailua-Kona
Dragon Inn Restaurant	Hilo
K. K. Tei Restaurant	Hilo
Reflections Restaurant	Hilo
Restaurant Fuji	Hilo
Rosey's Boathouse	Hilo
Roussels	Hilo/Waikoloa
S. S. James Makee	Keauhou
Spindrifter	Kailua-Kona
Sun Sun Lau	Hilo

If this is your first visit to The Big Island and you're afraid you missed all of the excitement don't worry. In the islands once a location becomes a restaurant spot it's almost always a restaurant spot. Hang around awhile and you'll discover that the table you're using may have once been occupied by Elvis and that before the Pacific Rim craze the place served Chinese! So get full value out of your stay by enjoying all that follows and discovering your own collection of old haunts.

Getting Around

At some point in their stay most adventurous Big Island visitors rent a car and take off on a road trip. This is a great way to see the sights, but before you start the engine there are a few things you should know. To begin with, unless you've been on the island before you'll probably need directions at some point. There are three distinctly different ways you'll see this done.

When you need help expect all of the following and often in combination:

1) The Mainland Method – ie, maps using route numbers, "Highway 11"

2) The Island Method – ie, signs using highway names, "Mamalahoa Highway"

3) The Local Method – ie, verbal using landmarks, "Go South Point"

Mainland visitors talk about going east or west. In the islands locals might say "Go Waipio" or "Go Kawaihae". Then, when directions do include a compass reference it's usually "Go West Side." On The Big Island this could also be said as "Go Kona Side". Expect multiple references in verbal directions. The locals might not know the route number, but they will know the town and destination.

Hawaii limits signage of all types to protect vistas. The signs that are permitted are physically small to deal with wind. In order to better get around determine the route number, name of the highway and your town and destination before starting out. If you get confused pull off the road to look at maps. Don't try to navigate and drive. Safety demands your full attention on the road and traffic.

The roads reflect the island territorial heritage. They follow geographical limits like shorelines rather than grids. Many have narrow right-of-ways and almost no shoulders. In remote areas one-lane bridges are common. The government has updated these roads, but physical realities restrict what can be done. Meanwhile some resist major changes to protect the old way of life and curb development.

If you get lost don't panic - you won't end up in Bangalore. When you're on an island and keep driving in the same direction you usually go all the way around and end up back in the same spot. Like most of the other Hawaiian Islands, the Big Island has loop roads that will bring you full circle. Follow the rules of the road - don't put everyone at risk by pulling a u-turn at a busy intersection.

Finally, remember that you're not the only one out there that's a bit perplexed. Hawaii has residents and visitors from all over the world. If you expect to see just about anything happen you won't be disappointed. Let your passengers do the sightseeing. If somebody spots a spouting whale or beautiful waterfall pull over and enjoy the scenery. Always drive akamai and stay safe in the islands!

Personal Favorites

He Said…She Said…We Said…

If there's something everyone wants to know it has to be, "What's your favorite restaurant?" That's a hard one to answer. There are dozens of great spots on The Big Island. Nevertheless, just like beauty is in the eye of the beholder, individual tastes and preferences mean everything when making this call. Having said that we have decided to hold up the bulls-eye and offer our list of personal favorites:

Bakery

He Said…	She Said…	We Said…
The Coffee Shack	Aloha Angel Cafe	The Coffee Shack

Burgers

He Said…	She Said…	We Said…
Quinn's	Drysdale's Two	Huggo's

Pizza

He Said…	She Said…	We Said…
Café Pesto	Kiawe Kitchen	Kona Pub & Brewery

Seafood

He Said…	She Said…	We Said…
Coast Grille	Sansei	Pahu i'a

Steak

He Said…	She Said…	We Said…
Kamuela Provision Co	Ruth's Chris	Ruth's Chris

Sushi

He Said…	She Said…	We Said…
Imari	Norio's	Sansei

Tacos

He Said…	She Said…	We Said…
Tako Taco	Tres Hombres	Los Habaneros

Tapas

He Said…	She Said…	We Said…
Kilauea Lodge	Merriman's Cafe	The Hualalai Grill

Asian
He Said...
Kenichi Pacific

She Said...
Kenichi Pacific

We Said...
Kenichi Pacific

Budget
He Said...
Ken's

She Said...
Bears Coffee

We Said...
Café 100

Exotic
He Said...
Thai Thai

She Said...
Rapanui Island Café

We Said...
Sushi Shiono

Family
He Said...
The Fish Hopper

She Said...
Big Island Grill

We Said...
Don's Grill

Fusion
He Said...
Daniel Thiebaut

She Said...
Hilo Bay Café

We Said...
Roy's at Waikoloa

Healthy
He Said...
Garden Snack Club

She Said...
Bamboo Restaurant

We Said...
Merriman's Restaurant

Island
He Said...
Nihon Restaurant

She Said...
Manago Hotel

We Said...
Seaside Restaurant

Local
He Said...
Blanes Drive Inn

She Said...
Nori's Saimin

We Said...
Hawaiian Style Café

Romantic
He Said...
Kona Inn

She Said...
Pescatore

We Said...
Pahu i'a

Views
He Said...
The Coffee Shack

She Said...
Ke'ei Cafe

We Said...
Don the Beachcomber

Waterfront
He Said...
Jameson's By The Sea

She Said...
Brown's Beach House

We Said...
Kona Inn

Family Friendly

Dining out was once reserved for business gatherings and special occasions. If someone wasn't getting married the kids stayed at home. Today, family outings to favorite restaurants have become a universal pastime. Likewise, travel is more democratic with everyone in the household participating. This brings us to every parent's dilemma, "Where do we eat when we're so far from home?"

We decided to develop a list of places we could recommend to families visiting The Big Island. Before making these selections we needed to create a yardstick. Everything in the islands has its own spin, so naturally what constitutes family friendly has to be determined by looking through an island lens. So forget the rules of proper behavior as proscribed by mainland morality and get on board!

To begin with if mom, pop and the kids are all going to The Big Island there are a bunch of airplane tickets to buy. Then, since the Hawaiian Islands are in the middle of the Pacific Ocean those tickets are going to be expensive. Take that and add on the cost of lodging and dad's wallet is probably going to be on life support. So the first rule we adopted was our selections had to be affordable.

Then we determined that since adult beverages are routinely available across the islands we would include places where they are served. Who cares what they are drinking at the next table? If you don't care to participate don't order anything! Smoking is banned in Hawaiian restaurants so that issue is moot. Add fun food and a relaxed atmosphere and you have the following recommendations:

Aloha Angel Cafe	Kainaliu
Bamboo Restaurant	Hawi
Big Island Grill	Kailua-Kona
Blanes Drive Inn	Hilo
Café 100	Hilo
Don's Grill	Hilo
Hawaiian Style Cafe	Waimea
Huli Sue's Barbeque	Waimea
Jackie Rey's Ohana Grill	Kailua-Kona
Ken's House of Pancakes	Hilo
Lava Rock Café	Volcano Village
Los Habaneros	Keauhou
Ocean Sushi	Hilo
Rapanui Island Cafe	Kailua-Kona
Royal Jade Garden	Kailua-Kona
Seaside Restaurant	Hilo
Solimene's	Waimea
Tako Taco	Waimea
Teshima Restaurant	Honalo
The Coffee Shack	Captain Cook

Luau Shows

Luaus are an integral part of the ancient Hawaiian culture. Today's visitors have the opportunity to attend luau shows that combine dining and entertainment on a scale only the Kamehamehas would have recognized. These extravagant events are usually limited to a few nights a week and come in a number of packages so we've chosen to list them and suggest that you contact the providers and ask for current relevant details. It's best to reserve in advance as many luaus book solid.

Hula Mana & Savai'i Luaus   North Kona
Kona Village Resort
Queen Ka'ahumanu Hwy (Hwy 19)
Kailua-Kona, HI 96740
808-325-5555

Island Breeze Luau   Kailua-Kona
King Kamehameha's Kona Beach Hotel
75-5660 Palani Road
Kailua-Kona, HI 96740
808-326-4969

Kamaha'o Luau   Keauhou
Sheraton Keauhou Bay Resort & Spa
78-128 Ehukai Street
Kailua-Kona, HI 96740
808-930-4900

Lava, Legends, and Legacies Luau   Kailua-Kona
Royal Kona Resort
75-5852 Ali'i Drive
Kailua-Kona, HI 96740
808-329-3111

Legends Of The Pacific Luau   South Kohala
Hilton Waikoloa Village
69-425 Waikoloa Beach Drive
Waikoloa, HI 96738
808-886-1234

Royal Luau   South Kohala
Waikoloa Beach Marriott Resort & Spa
69-275 Waikoloa Beach Drive
Waikoloa, HI 96738
808-886-6789

Watering Holes

Alcohol plays an interesting part in Hawaiian history. The missionaries abhorred it, the whalers wallowed in it and the rest of the population pretty much ignored it. Those who couldn't deal with alcohol are gone which leaves Hawaii squarely in the hands of people who don't see it as such a big deal. As a result beer, wine and assorted adult beverages are common features on menus across the islands.

Knowing that there are times when nothing else will do we would like to present a short list of possibilities. Understand that these are respectable establishments, they just so happen to have more of a focus on the good life than some others. If your minimal daily requirements include a cocktail hour you should feel right at home. Whether it's a quick drink or an evening's outing consider the following:

Café Pesto	Hilo & Kawaihae
Coast Grille	Kohala Coast
Drysdale's Two	Keauhou
Harbor House	Honokohau Harbor
Huggo's On The Rocks	Kailua-Kona
Jackie Rey's Ohana Grill	Kailua-Kona
Jameson's By The Sea	Kailua-Kona
Kamuela Provision Co	Waikoloa
Kenichi Pacific	Keauhou
Kona Inn	Kailua-Kona
Kona Pub & Brewery	Kailua-Kona
Lulu's	Kailua-Kona
Nihon Restaurant & Cultural Center	Hilo
Norio's	Kohala Coast
Quinn's Almost By The Sea	Kailua-Kona
Roy's Waikoloa Bar & Grill	Waikoloa
Sansei Seafood	Waikoloa
Seafood Bar	Kawaihae
Tommy Bahama's	Kohala Coast
Tres Hombres Beach Grill	Kawaihae

Before going out on the island be aware that mixed drinks are often served weak. This is especially true at luaus where the complimentary punch is usually longer on juice then "punch". Then to add insult to injury somebody forgot to tell many of the proprietors that people really CAN tell the difference between good liquor and cheap booze. Ask what's in the well – quality call pours cost very little more.

So make your visit to The Big Island whatever you want it to be. Everything has a proper time, and if it's adult time kick back and enjoy the good feelings, food and companionship. Just remember to have that really big night within walking distance of your hotel or with transportation provided by a designated driver. If good sense and all else fails remember that cabs are a lot cheaper than attorneys!

Quirks & Caveats

The farther one gets from something's origin the more likely it will take on a new identity. Since Hawaii is both geographically and culturally remote you can imagine the unique spins to be found in the islands. This shows up in all aspects of daily life but especially at the dinner table.

Let's start off with that ubiquitous condiment commonly known as soy sauce. In Hawaii soy sauce is called shoyu per the Japanese fashion. But wait, that doesn't mean that the Japanese version of soy sauce is preferred in Hawaii. No, the local taste runs to a lighter, sweeter product widely sold under the Aloha Shoyu label.

Like the Japanese, Hawaii people enjoy making teriyaki marinade with shoyu. Once again tastes change the recipe. In Japan teriyaki is a simple blend of soy sauce, rice wine and sugar, but in Hawaii the local Korean influence kicks in through the addition of green onions, garlic and ginger.

This takes us on to what constitutes salad. Mainland people have come to expect a combination of fresh vegetables and lettuces in their salads. That's not always the case in Hawaii. If the menu reads "toss salad" you can expect something you might recognize. However, if it reads "green salad" it probably means your meal comes with shredded cabbage while "salad" says get ready for mac and mayo.

Local tastes have put their stamp on meat dishes as well. Most Hawaii residents have Asian ancestry so those preferences naturally appear in entrees across the state. Choices like duck and lamb are common on Hawaii menus along with finfish of every description. On a lesser note boneless, skinless, chicken thighs hold forth in a thousand incarnations, some quite good, others best left alone.

Let's not forget red meat. Hawaii people are fond of beef and pork. A whole hog cooked imu style is everybody's favorite. But understand that this is a fatty dish which underscores the local taste for fat. You'll see fat everywhere from the top of a piece of Katsu chicken to the belly of a prime ahi tuna. Like anything fat is OK in moderation, but unless you want to live and look local pass some of it by.

As you travel about you'll see "barbeque" wherever you go. This doesn't mean what you might think. In most cases Hawaii barbeque is flame grilled, teriyaki marinated meat. Unlike mainland barbeque brush-on sauces, rubs and smoke don't enter in. That doesn't mean it isn't good, it just means it's different.

Finally, let's touch on an all important issue. In short, "Where's the restroom?" Like everything else in the islands the answer can be a little different. Of course the better places usually have excellent facilities, but when you decide to hit the strip malls and mom-and-pops anything becomes possible. If your quest takes you through the kitchen just say, "Hi!" and consider it part of the adventure.

Legend

Dress Code and Restaurant Price Symbols are based upon dinner. Lunch is usually a less expensive meal during which more casual attire is acceptable.

Restaurant Prices:

$	<$10
$$	$10-$25
$$$	$25-$40
$$$$	$40+

Credit Cards Accepted:

AE	American Express
CB	Carte Blanche
DC	Diners Club
DIS	Discover
JCB	Japan Credit Bank
MC	Master Card
V	Visa

Days of Operation:

Su	Sunday
Mo	Monday
Tu	Tuesday
We	Wednesday
Th	Thursday
Fr	Friday
Sa	Saturday
X	Except

Example: XMo = Every Day Except Monday

Dress Code:

Casual	t shirts, shorts, flip-flops, baseball hats
Resort Casual	shirt with a collar, shorts with pockets, sandals
Evening Aloha	long pants on gentlemen with closed-toed shoes
Formal	long sleeved dress shirt or jacket for gentlemen
Note:	Bathing suits and tank tops are suitable attire on the beach and by the pool. Cover-ups are a must at even the most casual of dining spots.

Rating System:

✓	Good	Meets acceptable standards
✓✓	Better	Exceeds usual requirements
✓✓✓	Superior	Great choice in most areas
✓✓✓✓	Excellent	Often the best to be found
✓✓✓✓✓	Exceptional	Rare and unique experience

In Hawaii it's considered poor manners to speak badly of someone. As the locals tell their children, "No talk stink!" With that in mind we resolved to avoid using negatives commonly associated with restaurant reviews. This put us on the high road of only including places we would return to and leaving out the rest. After that came the challenge of sorting out our newfound A list on a numerical scale.

We looked at several different approaches before settling on a five point system that allowed flexibility without bogging us down. Within this structure we view the four major factors of food, service, ambiance and value as equally important and scored accordingly. After comparing the establishments on our list with one another ratings were given creating what we hope is an accurate overall picture.

Menu Items:

Nothing in the world of travel changes faster than restaurant menus. Everything from the seasonal availability of local produce to which side of the bed the chef got up on impacts what you're offered when you sit down to dine. Nowhere will you find this more true than in Hawaii where the fresh catch of the day normally IS caught that day. If the boats didn't bring in opakapaka it just isn't available.

This guide attempts to help the reader come to his own conclusions. Menu items were chosen to give a well-rounded cross-section of the prospects and a sense of depth and complexity. Signature dishes have been included whenever offered as they tend to be constants and represent the chef's expertise and direction. Actual menu descriptions are used to best convey the mood and feel diners can expect.

Reservations:

It is always wise to call ahead as even the most established restaurateurs realign their meal service and hours periodically. Changes can almost be guaranteed in vacation destinations like Hawaii where life itself revolves around the seasons.

Spelling, Punctuation, & Pricing:

We have duplicated the spelling, punctuation and pricing as printed on menus in use at the time of publication. If you think some of them are unusual you should have seen what they did to our computer spell check and grammar programs! As prices are subject to change at anytime they should only be used as guidelines.

Hawaiian Islands

Kauai

Oahu

Molokai

Maui

Lanai

Kahoolawe

Hawaii

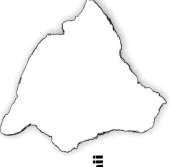

N
W E
S

ISLAND
CUISINES

Hawaiian Cuisine

Virtually everything and everybody in Hawaii came from someplace else which also holds true for many of the food sources we think of as native to the island chain. The Hawaiian Islands are geologically very young. They are also among the most remote places on earth with over twenty-five hundred miles of ocean separating the islands from any major land mass. Hawaii's youth and isolation led to the evolution of a unique but nutritionally sparse flora and fauna.

The first arrivals in Hawaii are thought to have been a small dark people whose origins hail back to Southeast Asia. Archaeologists believe that these people lived off what they found which didn't go much beyond fish, birds and a few native plants. Many like to think of those earliest inhabitants as the legendary Menehune, but they, like their history, disappeared into the annals of time. It wasn't until the Polynesians sailed to Hawaii with their domestic animals and "canoe" plants that the island food resources achieved any real variety.

These ancestors of the modern Hawaiians were great mariners. A thousand years ago early groups of explorers began sailing their double-hulled voyaging canoes up from Tahiti bringing along dogs, pigs and fowl to supplement their coconuts, sweet potatoes, breadfruit, bananas, taro, yams, arrowroot and sugarcane. They also brought the Polynesian approach to cooking which includes broiling over hot coals, boiling with hot stones and roasting in an underground oven. You'll find this latter method, cooking in an imu, holding center stage at luaus today.

Ancient Hawaiians lived in ahupua'a which were land divisions reaching from the top of the mountains down adjoining ridges to the ocean. These triangular watersheds theoretically contained all the resources required to sustain distinct communities. Trees for building canoes grew up on the mountain. The uplands supported dry land crops like sweet potatoes and yams. Down along the stream beds taro was grown in wet paddies called loi. Then, beyond the coconut and breadfruit trees lay the ocean with its wealth of fish, mollusks and seaweeds.

The Hawaiian diet was simple but healthful. Fish provided the majority of the common people's protein with domestic animals and fowl reserved primarily for the ruling class and special occasions. The staple starch was poi made from the steamed and pounded corms of the taro plant. When conditions wouldn't allow for taro cultivation sweet potatoes and breadfruit were used as substitutes. Taro greens and seaweed filled the need for leafy vegetables by supplying vitamins and minerals. Finally, bananas and coconuts were important for good health.

Today these traditions continue. Modern Hawaiians usually cook like everyone else, but they make it a point to hold luaus to celebrate milestones in life. Island favorites like kalua pig, lomi lomi salmon, chicken long rice, laulau, haupia and of course poi are staples at these events. If you get the chance attend a luau and experience the original Hawaiian cuisine.

23

Chinese Cuisine

The Chinese have influenced the socio-economic and culinary scenes of the islands to the point that it would be difficult to imagine Hawaii without them. Beginning in the mid 1800's they were the first immigrant group recruited to work in the sugarcane fields. From those humble beginnings the Chinese went on to become the merchant class and landlords of Honolulu.

The Chinese experience in Hawaii is more than a list of menu items and real estate investments. It's become an integral part of Hawaiian history. The early Chinese immigrants came from southern China, so naturally they brought that style of cooking with them. After they arrived it didn't take them long to figure out that there wasn't much of a future working on the plantations, so as soon as their contracts expired they moved on.

These free but unemployed farmers looked around and saw opportunity. Where the Hawaiians had once raised taro and fish the Chinese saw rice paddies and duck ponds. Intermarriage provided access to idle land that soon became truck gardens and small farms. Since trading is a way of life for all Chinese, the Port of Honolulu quickly had its own Chinatown full of shops and small eateries.

Today you see the effects of this history throughout the islands. The dominant Chinese cuisine in Hawaii is Cantonese. This is the style most visitors picture when they think about eating Chinese, so the methods and menu items are quite well known. Preparations like dim sum and stir-fries are popular in the region and are standards on menus in Hawaii.

True Chinese cooking is a healthful cuisine. Chefs in China instinctively strive for balance and harmony in meal preparation. This can be accomplished by using a variety of cooking methods and ingredients. No Chinese cook would ever serve an entire deep-fried meal; rather he or she would always include vegetable dishes and offer steamed rice on the side.

To fully enjoy a Chinese meal make sure you choose a variety of dishes, levels of spiciness and cooking methods. This is banquet style dining, but can still be done at a fairly reasonable cost. Some restaurants try to make things simpler by selecting an assortment of dishes and offering them as a package, but those set menus can be a bit on the middle-of-the-road side. Make your experience an adventure and select the items yourself - just watch out for the chicken feet!

No trip to Honolulu is complete without a visit to Chinatown. Take a walk and look for the shops with the barbequed pork and smoked ducks hanging in the windows. Down off King Street you'll find markets packed with people selling vegetables you've never seen and fish so fresh they're still swimming. Finally, stop for lunch at a place where you're the only ones speaking English and there isn't a fork in sight. That's when you'll know why they call it Chinatown.

Japanese Cuisine

Like so many others the Japanese experience in Hawaii is tied to sugar. The first immigrants began arriving from Japan soon after the end of the American Civil War. At first it was a trickle, but after the Reciprocity Act Of 1876 eliminated tariffs on Hawaiian sugar the trickle turned into a torrent. That was the age of industrialized sugar, and enormous amounts of manpower were required. Today Americans of Japanese ancestry play a major role in Hawaiian society. This is reflected through Hawaii's wide variety of Japanese dining venues.

Japanese diners eat with the eyes as well as their mouths. This becomes apparent after visiting one of their restaurants. Instead of a single main entrée dominating the table the Japanese prefer variety with smaller portions served separately on various sized plates and bowls artistically arranged around the table.

The ultimate fine dining experience is the kaiseki. This is also known as royal dining or dining in courses and involves considerable ceremony along with an elegant dinner presentation. An elaborate array of special courses is served that might include items such as an exquisite appetizer, assorted sashimi and sushi, miso soup, a tempura course, a seafood dish, a small steak, pickled vegetables, steamed rice, cold noodles and dessert.

A more common choice is the teishoku or complete meal. This is the Japanese equivalent of a prix fixe dinner consisting of an appetizer, miso soup, pickled vegetables, one or two entrees, rice and perhaps dessert. Anyone interested in exploring Japanese cuisine would do well to start with a teishoku as the variety allows the diner to do some sampling and not be overwhelmed by the menu.

Within the various meal presentations you'll find a variety of preparation styles. Thanks to the spread of international dining island visitors often think of sushi and sashimi as typical Japanese food. While those are popular dishes in Japan their cuisine goes far deeper than that. Beyond the temptations of the sushi bar you will find several major styles of cooking.

First comes yakimono, which are grilled or broiled dishes. Teriyaki and yakitori are classic examples of yakimono. The knife-wielding showman in a teppanyaki steak house is also doing a form of yakimono cooking. Then you'll see agemono where meats or vegetables are fried in oil. Tempura with its light, puffy coating is probably the most recognizable form of agemono. Finally, discover nabemono where thinly sliced pieces of meat and vegetables are individually simmered in a fragrant broth using a tabletop chaffing dish. Both shabu shabu and sukiyaki are traditional nabemono dishes.

It doesn't matter if you are a culinary newcomer or an old hand, just stroll into a Japanese restaurant with confidence and after a half-bow to the hostess get ready for a truly unique and exceptional dining experience.

25

Portuguese Cuisine

Portuguese culinary tradition has always been the odd-man-out among Hawaiian ethnic cuisines. Where the others have Asian origins, Portuguese is European. If the Asians serve a starch it is nearly always rice. For the Portuguese starch says bread or beans. Asians love stir-fries. The Portuguese prefer stews. In spite of all this, Portuguese cooking has become a valued part of the island melting pot.

The Portuguese have always been a seafaring people. During the fourteenth and fifteenth centuries Portuguese sailors embarked on a wave of global exploration. Those adventurers brought back spices and foods that were unknown in Europe. The resulting trade routes reached around the world exposing the Portuguese to exotic places and exotic places to the Portuguese.

The first Portuguese plantation laborers arrived in Hawaii during the 1870's and were actually from the Azores and Madeira. This was a natural development as sugarcane had been part of the Madeira agricultural scene for hundreds of years. These European immigrants differed from their Asian cohorts as they intended to stay in Hawaii permanently. Their families brought hearth and home along with the entire range of Portuguese cuisine.

Hearty soups, stews and casseroles were a rather new concept in the islands but old favorites among the Portuguese. They were usually enhanced with the wide variety of spices and flavors that had come into their possession through global exploration. Portuguese sausage or linguica with its garlicky zest has gone on to become a mainstay breakfast item across the islands. In Hawaii you'll see eggs and Portuguese sausage right next to Egg McMuffins and breakfast burritos on fast food restaurant menus.

Another island favorite is Portuguese Bean Soup. If Hawaii people had to name the recipes that make their top ten list, Portuguese Bean Soup would be present every time. Somehow it doesn't seem to matter what kind of menu a restaurant normally serves or where its price range falls this local comfort food combining beans and vegetables with ham hocks and Portuguese sausage usually manages to make its way into the rotation as Soup of the Day.

Finally, there is the Portuguese tradition of baking bread. Everywhere you go in Hawaii you'll find menus offering French toast made with Portuguese sweet bread. Also known as pao doce, this local favorite has taken on another identity as Molokai Sweet Bread. Visitors to that island will see local people boarding their plane carrying loaves for those at home. Another Portuguese specialty is a sugary doughnut without a hole known as the malasada. Traditionally served as a special treat the day before Ash Wednesday, malasadas were prepared using the family's remaining butter and eggs before starting the lean times of Lent.

Korean Cuisine

Immigrants from Korea began arriving in Hawaii during the early 1900's. Like their fellows the early arrivals came to work on the plantations. Although that era is all but over, the migration continues today as Koreans seeking economic opportunity leave their homeland for Hawaii and other parts of North America.

Koreans strive for balance and harmony in all aspects of their lives. This is quite obvious at dinnertime where they look at food as a cure for physical and mental ailments as well as for sustenance. Their cuisine is low in fat and very healthful with an emphasis on grilled or broiled meats, soups and fresh vegetables. Some of the cooking methods favored by Koreans involve tableside preparation using a grill or by simmering in broth, while others require pan or deep-frying.

One item that has almost come to mean Korean is kim chee. Interestingly, both of this pickled relish's principal ingredients came from other places. The Dutch introduced cabbage to the Koreans and the chili peppers that give kim chee its fire were brought from Portugal. This zesty condiment is nearly always seen on Korean tables and adds zip to offset the mildness of rice.

Contrary to general impressions not all Korean food is highly seasoned. In fact, many of their favorite dishes could easily pass as comfort food. If people enjoy teriyaki then they'll appreciate the marinated grilled meats. Koreans are more of a beef-eating nation than most other Asian countries. It is thought that invading Mongols introduced cattle to Korea hundreds of years ago. Other protein sources common to the Korean diet include poultry and fish as well as soybean products.

For those who really must know all the details some of the ingredients used as flavoring in Korean cuisine include chrysanthemum leaves, daikon, ginger root, garlic, enokitake, shimeji and shiitake mushrooms, hot green and red peppers, green onions, mirin, miso, nori, sesame oil and seeds, pine nuts, soybean sprouts, soy sauce, tofu and wakame.

Combination meals are usually offered giving the diner a chance to experience a variety of items. These dinners begin with a variety of small dishes containing salads and pickled vegetables. Turnips, potatoes, kim chee, seaweed, garlic bulb pickles and bean sprouts among others might be offered. Soups made of oxtails, fish, chicken or vegetables, many times with the addition of beaten egg and/or dumplings are important courses in a Korean meal. Popular entrées commonly seen include bulgoki, kal bi ribs and chun. As usually found in Asian cuisines, desserts are limited to fruits and special occasion items.

Most island Korean restaurants tend to be less formal establishments where one can enjoy a healthful dinner of wonderfully prepared foods at a reasonable cost. We heartily recommend this experience to the travel adventurers whose agenda includes getting off the beaten track and rubbing elbows with the locals.

Filipino Cuisine

Filipinos constituted the last major immigrant group recruited to work Hawaii's sugarcane and pineapple plantations. Their arrival during the early to mid 1900's was a reaction to legal restrictions placed by the US government on bringing in foreign workers. The Hawaiian plantations needed cheap field labor, and as the Philippines were a US territory, it became the logical alternative.

Although at first glance one might assume that the Philippine culture would be Southeast Asian in nature that is not at all the case. Early trading visits from the east followed by three hundred years of Spanish occupation and fifty years as a US territory heavily influenced Filipino daily life. The result is truly global.

Seafaring merchants from China and Malaysia are thought to have been the first outsiders to seriously impact the culinary traditions of the Philippine archipelago. The use of egg roll wrappers in lumpia, rice, curry, coconut, coconut milk, patis, soy sauce and noodles all appear to have had their origins in eastern cuisines.

Then came the Spanish whose presence truly made an impression on the daily diet in the Philippines. Tomatoes, onion, garlic, beans, pimientos and olive oil have become everyday components in Filipino dishes. During the late 1890's America was at war with Spain and the islands came under US military control. Although Filipino people enjoy American dishes as well as their own, little of what we consider true Filipino food can be attributed to that period of history.

Today the Filipino influence on the culinary tradition in Hawaii might not be as noticeable as that of some other Asian cuisines as Main Street restaurants don't commonly serve an exclusively Filipino menu. However, that doesn't mean that visitors won't be exposed to Filipino food. Many island restaurants incorporate Filipino styles and dishes in their lineup. You just have to know where to look.

Filipino cooks like to blend all of the ingredients in a meal together rather than preparing and serving them separately. A classic example of this is adobo, which is a stew made from pork and/or chicken that have been marinated in garlic and vinegar. Another is chicken relleno, which is a roasted and boned chicken that is stuffed with a pork, onion, raisin, pimiento and hard-cooked egg stuffing.

Then come the veggies! Filipino tradition calls for the use of an extremely wide variety of vegetables. Most Western visitors won't easily identify many of them, but a walk through an Asian grocery or Chinatown will give you the picture. Of course, no meal would be complete without rice or pancit noodles on every plate.

Finally, Filipino people are fond of sweets. Look for leche flan, fruit lumpia or cascaron and you'll know you've found the dessert section of the menu. Move a little farther off the main drag and you just might find halo-halo. This refreshing island milkshake is made with ice, coconut milk and tasty fruit surprises.

Thai Cuisine

Thais were among the first immigrants to Hawaii who didn't come seeking work on the plantations. Their arrival over the last forty years was part of a movement out of Southeast Asia by those seeking greater economic opportunity. As many before them had already discovered a quick way to generate an income in a new land is to open a restaurant and introduce the neighborhood to your homeland's cuisine. Hawaii with its sizeable Asian ethnic population was a natural for these new entrepreneurs. Thai cuisine got rave reviews and quickly become a favorite.

Thai cuisine reflects an interesting history of interaction between people through out Indochina. Thanks to its central location Thailand became a crossroad for foreign travelers and exotic ideas. Immediately to the north lies China with its ancient traditions of stir-frying and the use of noodles. Among that group were Buddhists preparing vegetarian dishes. From the west came people from India making curries and Arabs cooking skewer-broiled meats. And of course don't forget the ever-present Portuguese and their tiny red hot peppers!

Chefs from Thailand have a whole arsenal of flavors at their disposal. Some of the ingredients commonly used include Thai chilies; Kaffir lime leaves, ginger, lemongrass, mint, basil, curry, peppers and the ever-present fish sauce known as nam pla. Thai food may be ordered spiced mild, medium or hot. However, since mild dishes can miss the point and hot is best reserved for the Thai's we suggest that people consider ordering medium. Then, in order to moderate the hot, spicy flavors be sure to include at least one dish that includes coconut milk and have it all served along side a steamer basket of Thai sticky rice.

Thai restaurants usually serve meals all at once rather than in courses. A number of dishes are presented giving everyone an opportunity to sample the full variety of items. Great effort is made to balance out the contrasting tastes and textures in order to promote harmony in the meal. In contrast to many Asian countries, a fork and spoon are used when dining. The fork is used for cutting and pushing food onto the spoon, while the spoon helps the diner fully appreciate the sauces.

A good rule to follow when making menu selections is to always ask, "What do the regulars order?" Naturally there are favorites like anywhere else. Starting off with the appetizer section consider the Thai Crispy Noodles or Satay Chicken. Then follow up with a Green Papaya Salad and a party-size bowl of Tom Yum Soup. Next comes the main event where dishes like Evil Prince Shrimp, Pork Pad Pet, Chicken Panang Curry and Beef with Thai Basil Sauce appear high on every list. Finally, include a platter of Pad Thai Noodles and dinner is served.

Try to visit a Thai restaurant while in you're in Hawaii. Ask for ordering advice if you need it or go it alone as you see fit. Regardless, you're a lot closer to the land the Thais call home, and that puts you in a position to discover an exciting new cuisine that truly broadens the horizons of culinary adventure.

Vietnamese Cuisine

The end of the Vietnam War signaled the beginning of a major migration out of Southeast Asia to Hawaii and North America. What began as a political exodus turned into a classic movement of people seeking a better way of life. The island state with its temperate climate and the presence of other Asian cultures became an attractive resettlement destination that draws Vietnamese immigrants to this day. Their presence has become so visible that there are those who refer to the central part of Honolulu's Chinatown historic district as Little Saigon.

While you are walking around Chinatown notice the small Vietnamese eateries that seem to be popping up on every street corner. At one time immigrants from China operated these shops. Now those people have moved on to other pursuits and the latest wave of arrivals have taken their place. Many of these places are pho shops. Pho is pronounced "fuh" and is an aromatic rice noodle soup made with a clear, rich beef stock. Fresh herbs such as Thai basil and cilantro along with bean sprouts and jalapeños are served alongside on a separate plate. The diners then flavor this popular dish to their own specifications.

Vietnamese cuisine is the result of many years of cultural blending. Like the other countries in Southeast Asia, the ebb and flow of history brought them successive waves of new multitudes and customs. The original inhabitants of Vietnam are thought to have moved down the coastline from southern China. Then newcomers from the east and west arrived looking for trade. There were occupations, first by the Chinese and then by the French. Throughout that time the people of Vietnam were learning new culinary methods and techniques.

As you peruse a Vietnamese menu you will witness those influences through the use of everything from croissants and baguettes to lemongrass and curry paste. Naturally, the Asian staple starch appears as a major item. Not only do you see rice served steamed as a side dish, but it also appears in noodles and as rice paper for wrapping. Vietnamese foods have a delicate fresh taste and are never heavy in texture or flavor. Herbs are used as greens as well as for flavor. Dishes made with curry may be ordered spiced according to your preference.

A Vietnamese meal is served family style where everyone samples each dish. Preparation is not a detailed or complicated endeavor, but rather a gathering of fresh healthful ingredients handled and cooked as little as possible. A favorite example is the banh hoi. This popular dish is made by taking grilled marinated meat slices and placing them on a moist rice paper wrapper piled with pickled daikon, carrots, bean sprouts, romaine, rice vermicelli and fresh mint leaves. This is then rolled up like a burrito and dipped into a light, flavorful sauce.

Vietnamese cuisine is the new kid on Hawaii's culinary block. Although some of the surroundings may be a little basic go on in and try this wonderful taste experience just once and you will find yourself wanting to go back for more!

Local Food

Local food is the Hawaiian Everyman's version of homegrown comfort food. Its roots go back to the plantation days when people were recruited from around the world to work the sugarcane and pineapple fields. Although they were quartered in separate camps based upon nationality, the workers gathered in small groups at lunchtime, and that is where the blending of cultures began.

The field workers' diet was pretty simple. Just about everyone had a tin of rice and some kind of meat and vegetable. A Japanese worker might bring teriyaki beef, and his Portuguese cohort would probably pack a can of sardines. Figure that the Koreans will bring along some kim chee while the Filipinos surely had adobo or lumpia. Then, in a kind of Hawaiian potluck the workers would share what they brought bringing variety to an otherwise ordinary lunch in the field.

That was the beginning of local food, but what does it look like today? When you think local food imagine something simple a plantation family would keep in their pantry. First comes the staple starch, which is nearly always rice. Then you have canned meat of which Spam, Vienna Sausages, sardines, corned beef and beef stew predominate. To add a little interest there would be a jar of mayo and a bag of macaroni with which to make a simple mac salad. Then the farmer would bring his cabbage down from upcountry and dinner would be served.

Most visitors to Hawaii experience local food at one of the lunch counters seen just about everywhere in the islands. The standard offering is commonly called plate lunch. For seven or eight dollars you get a choice of meat such as teriyaki chicken, katsu pork or mahi mahi, "two scoop" rice and a scoop of mac salad. The whole affair comes appropriately served in a Styrofoam carryout container complete with plastic table service. Bon Appetit!

If a steaming bowl of noodle soup is more your style local food accommodates as well. The staple item here is known as saimin. This dish has an interesting history. The Chinese say it has a Japanese origin and the Japanese say it came from China, so they both must be right! To make saimin first you must have a stock. In the Japanese tradition this would be a dashi which is broth made from nori flavored with bonito shavings. Since this is a little lean for many tastes the choices take off from there. Some places use chicken stock while others include pork bones in as well. Determining personal preference and figuring out who is using what is part of the adventure of exploring the local food establishments.

Don't forget the noodles that by tradition are made from wheat flour, water, and eggs. This "long rice" is complemented with a little meat and perhaps an egg as well as some Chinese cabbage to top the whole thing off. Local types will buy a teri-beef stick or two to add flavor to their bowl or as a side dish with a touch of hot mustard. We recommend beginning your saimin experience just as it arrives from the kitchen before adding a dash of hoisin or Tabasco sauce for extra zest.

Pacific Rim Cuisine

In a geographical sense Pacific Rim refers to all of the nations that border the Pacific Ocean. This area not only includes Japan, Korea, China and Southeast Asia but also takes in Australia, New Zealand and all of Polynesia as well as South, Central and North America. However, no matter how large that seems physically in a cultural sense the Pacific Rim involves even that much more.

People from diverse cultures have shared culinary traditions since the beginning of time. This interaction greatly accelerated as worldwide commercial activity, improved communications and personal travel experiences impacted the general public. During the 20th century our new awareness of different culinary practices began to change people's expectations regardless of economic status. Witness the evolving trends in the American dietary culture as we went from Italian and Chinese to Mexican and Thai. Once we began to sample we didn't want to stop.

This brings us to a better understanding of the dynamics behind the Pacific Rim movement. Watching the explosion of mass-produced ethnic convenience foods what enterprising young chef wouldn't try to capitalize on a new trend? Taking advantage of opportunity, professional chefs began using their classic training to blend ingredients from one group of countries and preparation methods from another to produce results that are on a higher level than the sum of the parts.

For instance, grilled beef tenderloin with shiitake mushrooms in a Marsala demi glace served with mashed Hawaiian taro and Okinawan sweet potatoes is a far cry from a grilled steak and baked potato. The combination utilizes Hawaiian, Chinese, French, Italian, Okinawan, Continental European and American foods and methods to elevate the diner's experience. The chef's formal training and experience in blending flavors led to the resulting balanced and pleasing entree.

In the Hawaiian Islands travelers sometimes wonder if they are being offered Pacific Rim or Hawaii Regional Cuisine. Hawaii Regional Cuisine showcases locally produced fish, meats, fruits and vegetables combined with local ethnic styles and classic cooking techniques to create an upscale, contemporary version of Hawaiian "local food". Pacific Rim Cuisine draws upon a much broader area when sourcing ingredients and cooking methods while producing an innovative fusion of cuisines from all around the Pacific Rim.

A visit to a Pacific Rim restaurant is like a trip to a foodie theme park. As you read the menu try and picture the tastes and ingredients the chef is combining before you make your selection. Not all the world's flavors and textures are to everyone's liking. By thinking about what you really enjoy and then following your own lead you will be much better prepared to select those dishes most likely to please so you can experience a truly enjoyable dining experience.

Hawaii Regional Cuisine

There was a time when fine dining in Hawaii was a less than stellar experience. Much of what appeared on the restaurant menus had to be shipped in over long distances. Anything that could be shipped frozen and whatever couldn't arrived tired. Then, in order to try and please the visitors, the local chefs tried to prepare classic cuisine under less than ideal circumstances. As you can imagine, cooking Continental out of a can didn't work very well.

Along came the late 1980's and a group of young chefs decided that something had to be done to improve the situation. They began talking with local farmers, fishermen and ranchers about the types of products needed to raise the level of their culinary offerings. Then, in order to create new and exciting dishes these chefs began merging local cultural influences with their newfound sources of supply, and Hawaii Regional Cuisine was on its way to being born

In the original group there were twelve chefs who banded together and formally created the Hawaii Regional Cuisine movement. Those twelve were: Sam Choy, Roger Dikon, Mark Ellman, Bev Gannon, Jean Marie Josselin, George (Mavro) Mavrothalassitis, Peter Merriman, Amy Ferguson Ota, Philippe Padovani, Alan Wong and Roy Yamaguchi. It was their goal to combine fresh island products with local ethnic cooking styles and classic techniques to create a contemporary upscale regional cuisine exclusive to Hawaii.

Hawaii Regional Cuisine is a fusion of elements from both eastern and western cultures. Much of the inspiration then comes from the simple beginnings of the plantation camps and what islanders call "local food". Add that to an innovative group of classically trained chefs and the freshest of local products and you get truly unique preparations unlike anything you've ever experienced.

There are an amazing variety of offerings on a Hawaii Regional Cuisine menu. Naturally, fresh island fish like opakapaka and mahi-mahi appear regularly, but so do local aquaculture products like Kahuku prawns and Keahole lobster. Look for the Asian preparations and Polynesian sauces that take these specialties one-step beyond. Then to complement the seafood dishes you might find innovative items like pineapple chicken or macadamia crusted lamb rounding things out.

While you are traveling in the islands keep an eye out for restaurants operated by any of the twelve original Hawaii Regional Cuisine chefs. They will surely provide you with a memorable evening of dining enjoyment. There's also a new group of young up and coming chefs who are doing wonderful work in Hawaii. They call themselves the Hawaiian Island Chefs and include Steve Ariel, Chai Chaowasaree, Hiroshi Fukui, Teri Gannon, George Gomes, Wayne Hirabayashi, D. K. Kodama, Lance Kosaka, Jacqueline Lau, Douglas Lum, James McDonald, Mark Okumura, Russell Siu, Goren Streng and Corey Waite. Look for them as you choose your next dining spot. They're the new wave and they're here today.

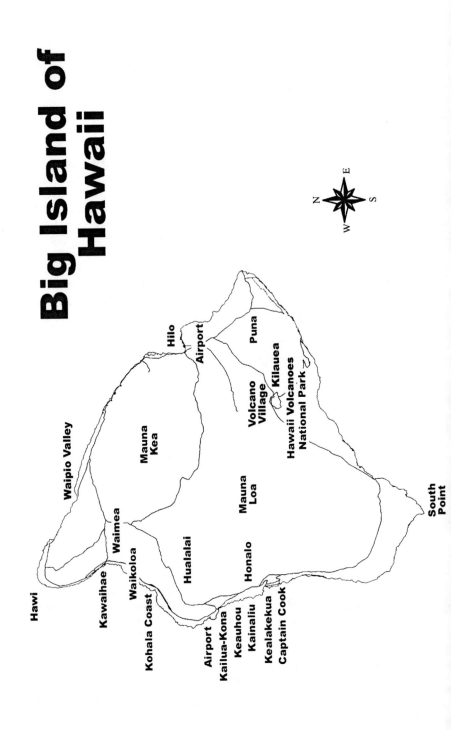

BIG ISLAND
OF HAWAII
DINING

Big Island Dining

Kona

Aloha Angel Café ✓✓
79-7384 Mamalahoa Hwy (Hwy 11)
Kainaliu, HI 96750
808-322-3383
www.alohatheatre.com

Hours: BL 7:00 AM-2:30 PM
        D 5:00 PM-8:30 PM on Theater Nights
Cards: AE JCB MC V
Dress: Resort Casual
Style: Innovative Island $$

Menu Sampler: Kids Menu Too

Breakfast/Lunch:
All egg dishes served with garlic red potatoes or rice and choice of multi-grain toast or homemade cornbread, Surfer Special of two eggs your way, choice of bacon, ham, Portuguese or vegetable sausage links $9.95, 3 Egg Omelette or Scramble with spinach, mushrooms & cheese $10.95, French toast made with Hawaiian sweet bread $6.50, Fresh Fish of the day & Eggs $12.95, Chinese Salad of soba noodles, grilled tofu or chicken, cucumbers, bean sprouts & snow peas tossed in house creamy sesame dressing with crispy wontons on a bed of greens $12.95, Burger includes choice of chips, garlic red potatoes $9.95, Chicken or Tofu Tacos with island greens and chipotle sauce $11.95, Fresh Island Fish Sandwich grilled or blackened on Kaiser roll, tomato, red onion with choice of Maui chips, homemade potato mac salad or garlic red potatoes $12.95

Dinner:
Appetizers: New Zealand Green Lipped Mussels $9.95, Shrimp Scampi $10.95
Entrées: served with vegetables and choice of potatoes or rice du jour, Fresh Catch of the Day $22.95, Lamb chops $24.95, 10 oz. Grilled Rib Eye Steak $21.95, Calamari Steak with house lemon caper sauce $17.95, Coconut Lemongrass Yellow Curry with Chicken or Tofu $17.95. Hokulani Pasta in garlic, butter, white wine, tomatoes, artichoke hearts and basil $17.95
Adult Beverages: Beer/Wine Cellar/Cocktails – Corkage Fee $5.00

Impressions: Plantation Days

This trendy café/bakery offers an eclectic breakfast and lunch menu out on their picturesque south lanai and a more traditional dinner in the nearby dining room. Prices are affordable by nearly any standard, and the bakery features wonderful homemade goodies and Kona Coffee for those on their way to the volcano. It's all done in the historic Aloha Theater building where entertainment in the form of movies, plays and concerts is still provided regularly. Imagine "Old Hawaii".

Kohala Coast

Bamboo Restaurant & Gallery ✓✓✓
Old Takata Store
Akoni Pule Hwy (Hwy 270)
Hawi, HI 96719
808-889-5555
www.bamboorestaurant.info

Hours: Bru 11:30 AM-2:30 PM Su
            L 11:30 AM-2:30 PM Tu-Sa
            D 6:00 PM-7:30 PM Tu-Th
            D 6:00 PM-8:00 PM Fr-Sa
Cards: DC MC V
Dress: Casual
Style: Pacific Rim $$

Menu Sampler:　　　　　　　Kids Menu Too

Brunch:
Eggs Bamboo with lilikoi hollandaise sauce, one egg 5.95/two eggs 7.95, most brunch entrees are under 9.95, Fresh Island Fish Special - Market Price

Lunch:
Kohala Coconut Grilled Chicken with Thai coconut sauce served on fresh vegetables & steamed rice 8.95, Kohala Quesadillas with kalua pork 8.95, Teri Chicken Sandwich 8.75, BBQ Pork sandwich 8.75

Dinner:
Pupus: Chicken Sate Pot Stickers of seasoned chicken, herbs and peanuts wrapped in won ton pi, steamed and served with sweet chili mint sauce 7.95
Entrées: Beef Tenderloin grilled to your taste and finished w/Jack Daniel's "Tipsy" Sauce 19.95/29.95, Macadamia Nut Crusted Chicken Cordon Bleu of chicken breasts wrapped around Kalua pork & Swiss cheese, seared, then topped with lilikoi mustard drizzle 24.95, Fresh Island Fish Special - Market Price
Adult Beverages: Beer/Wine Cellar/Cocktails – Corkage Fee 15.00

Impressions:　　　　　　　Special Spot

There aren't many deserted highways left in the islands, but there IS one you won't want to miss. Head north up the Kohala Coast and experience a hidden Hawaiian scenic treasure. Near the end of the road you'll come to the historic plantation town of Hawi. There inside an old hotel turned general store you'll find Bamboo with its eclectic blend of island and Asian cuisines. Convention doesn't mean much on this side of paradise so don't look for the resort dining room formula of all things for all people. Instead, those lucky enough to make the trip will find a kitchen that's in perfect balance with the alternative setting.

Hilo

Bears' Coffee ✓✓
106 Keawe Street
Hilo, HI 96720
808-935-0708
Web: None
Hours: BL 7:00 AM-4:00 PM Mo-Fr
       BL 7:00 AM-1:00 PM Sa
       BL 7:00 AM-12:00 PM Su
Cards: None
Dress: Casual
Style: Deli $

Menu Sampler: Kids Menu Too

Breakfast:
Two Souffléd Eggs steamed in an espresso machine with choice of toast 3.25, choice of ten toppings at additional cost, Ham Buster one egg cooked with ham and cheddar cheese 4.00, Belgian Waffles 4.00, with fruit and whipped cream 5.00, Lox & Bagel with cream cheese, sweet red onion, tomato and lemon 7.00
Bakery Delights: Muffins 1.60, Bears' Cinnamon Roll - Bear Size 2.50, Bear Paws 2.50, Bagel 'N Peanut Butter 2.50, Cheese Croissant 2.75, Croissant 2.00
Drinks: Coffee of the Day $1.60, Espresso $1.75/$2.00, Café Mocha 3.25, Café Latte 3.00, Mexican Coffee 3.25, Almond Milk 2.50, Cappucino 2.75
Lunch:
Greek Salad - fresh greens, feta cheese, Greek olives, sweet red onions, Greek peppers, pepperoncini 6.00, Soup of the Day 3.00/bowl, Choice of bagel 1.75, choice of various toppings .40 to1.95 each, Deli Sandwiches of Turkey, Hot Pastrami, Ham, Egg Salad, Chicken Filet, Tuna, Garden, Super Cheesy Melt with choice of bread 4.95, Bears' Pizza – vegetarian or pepperoni 5.00
Adult Beverages: N/A
Dinner:
N/A

Impressions: Cozy Cafe

Hilo people have to go to work like everybody else, but since this is Hawaii and things move a little slower in the islands the local coffee shop doesn't open until 7AM. After that, progress takes over with the kitchen turning out breakfast items at a steady pace until the regulars have all gone their way. Meanwhile the rest of us kick back and enjoy a cup of nature's finest. Bears' is a traditional small town café serving good quality, value-oriented food and beverages seven-days-a-week.

Big Island Dining

Kona

Big Island Grill ✓
75-5702 Kuakini Highway
Kailua-Kona, HI 96740
808-326-1153
Web: None
Hours: B 6:00 AM-11:00 AM
          L 11:00 AM-5:00 PM
          D 5:00 PM-9:00 PM
Cards: DIS MC V
Dress: Casual
Style: American $$

Menu Sampler:

Breakfast:
Hawaiian Style French Toast 6.25, Belgian Waffles with strawberries or blueberries 8.00, Two Eggs, Meat Choice, Hash Browns, Rice or Toast 8.75, Build Your Own Omelet 9.75, Pork Chops & Eggs 11.75, Eggs Benedict 9.50
Lunch:
Chicken Salad stuffed into a half papaya 8.75, Coconut Shrimp Salad on greens with plum chili sauce and creamy sesame 13.25, Roast Beef Sandwich 9.75, Hot Roast Pork Sandwich 9.75, Fried Chicken 11.25, Fresh Island Catch sautéed or broiled with choice of fries, rice, mashed potatoes and fresh vegetables Market, Plate lunches w/choice of local entrée, starch, salad or vegetables 9.25 to 11.25
Dinner:
Baby Back Ribs w/house hoisin guava BBQ sauce 19.75, Chicken Picatta with lemon, butter, capers, garlic, white wine 16.25, Rib Eye Steak with choice of soup or tossed salad and choice of mashed potatoes, rice or fries with fresh vegetables 20.50, BIG Burger 8.25, add mushrooms, bacon onions 1.50 each, Shrimp Scampi with garlic, white wine and butter 18.25, Pork Chops 15.25
Desserts: Hawaiian Mud Pie 6.00, Sweet Potato Haupia Cheesecake 6.00, Banana Cream Pie 4.75, Apple or Cherry Pie 4.50, add scoop ice cream 1.75
Adult Beverages: BYO Wine – No Corkage Fee

Impressions: Bustling Diner

Big Island Grill is a favorite dining spot among the Kailua-Kona townsfolk. Its location in a former fast-food restaurant makes for plenty of seating area and a reasonable amount of parking. In keeping with all this, the décor could best be described as efficient. The extensive menu revolves around reasonably priced American standards. Things can get a bit hectic here, but the staff keeps things moving. Expect home-style meals served three times a day, seven days a week.

Big Island Dining

Blanes Drive Inn ✓✓
217 Waianuenue Avenue
Hilo, HI 96720
808-969-9494
Web: None
Hours: B 5:00 AM-10:30 AM
LD 5:00 AM-9:00 PM
Cards: MC V
Dress: Casual
Style: Local $

Additional Locations

150 Wiwoole Street
Hilo, HI 96720
808-935-2259

16-127 Orchidland Drive
Hilo, HI 96720
808-982-9800

Menu Sampler: **Kids Menu Too**

Breakfast:
Regular Breakfast comes with choice of bacon, Spam, Portuguese sausage, ham, luncheon meat, link sausage, corned beef hash or hamburger patty and rice, hashbrowns or toast $4.25, Banana Pancake $4.00, Omelette $4.75
Lunch/Dinner:
Plate Lunches: regular plate includes 2 scoops rice and mac or toss salad, mini includes 1 scoop rice and mac salad, free miso soup on request w/regular plate, Hamburger Steak $7.00/$5.75, Boneless Chicken or Roast Pork $7.25/$6.00, Grilled Chicken Breast $8.50/$7.25, , Mahi Mahi or Roast Beef $7.50/$6.25
Locos: bowl or plate, Hamburger or Teri Hamburger$4.00/$7.50, Boneless Chicken or Roast Pork $4.75/$8.25, Mahi Mahi, or Roast Beef $5.00/ $8.50
Bentos: Mix Bento (boneless chicken, teri beef, luncheon meat) $5.00, Mahi Deluxe Bento (mahi, boneless chicken, teri beef, luncheon meat) $6.25
Chowders & Combos: alternate daily, Clam Chowder $3.50/$4.25, Corn Chowder $3.25/$4.00, Sandwich or Salad and Chowder $5.25 to $6.95
Homemade Burgers: single or double, Hamburger $2.00/$3.25, Gravy Burger $2.20/$3.45, Cheese Burger $2.25/$3.50, Teri Burger $2.20/$3.45, Deluxe $.50
Sandwiches: Mahi or Grilled Ahi $3.75, Pastrami 6" $4.00, Philly Cheese Steak or Grilled Chicken Breast 6" $4.25, BLT $3.00, Grilled Tuna & Cheese $3.00
Saimin Noodles: small or large, Saimin or Fried Saimin $3.00/$5.50, Saimin Deluxe $3.25/$6.00, Dry Saimin Deluxe $3.75/$7.00, Noodle Special $6.25
Adult Beverages: N/A

Impressions: **Picnic Style**

Old-fashioned drive-ins may have been displaced on the mainland, but they are alive and well in Hilo. Blanes does it right with good food and affordable prices. We were particularly impressed with the quality of the fish sandwiches. They're what we remember before fish became rectangular. Lots of cover for rainy days.

Big Island Dining

Kohala

Brown's Beach House ✓✓✓
The Fairmont Orchid, Hawaii
One North Kaniku Drive
Kohala Coast, HI 96743
808-885-2000
www.fairmont.com/orchid
Hours: D 5:30 PM-8:30 PM
Cards: AE DC DIS JCB MC V
Dress: Resort Casual
Style: Island $$$

Menu Sampler: Kids Menu Too

Breakfast/Lunch:
N/A
Dinner:
Appetizers: Hamakua Mushrooms En Croute 16, Dungeness Crab Cakes with Waimea Corn Sauce, Coconut Red Curry Sauce and roasted corn relish 21
Salads: Ahi Poke with Hawaiian sea salt, yuzu, sesame oil, Maui onion, chives, chili paste, shoyu, limu, sesame lavosh, cucumber and daikon chips 21, House Caesar Salad with cured Ahi, sesame lavosh, Parmigiano reggiano 16
Soups: Paauilo Vanilla Keahole Lobster Bisque, crisp taro 16, Coconut Seafood Tom Yum Soup with shrimp, calamari, diver scallops, Hawaiian fish, coconut broth, ginger, lemongrass, Kaffir lime, coconut chilies 21
Entrées: Fresh Linguine with Big Island Goat Cheese, pear tomato and garlic herb sauce, roasted Kobacha pumpkin puree 28, Roast Kurobata Pork Tenderloin wrapped with applewood smoked bacon and leeks, liliko'i brandy sauce, shrimp fried rice, seasonal vegetables 36, Mahogany Glazed Tofu 26
Desserts: Tropical Fruit Gazpacho with yogurt panna cotta 11, Baked Hawaiian Chocolate Mousse Cake with banana ice cream and caramel sauce, roasted mac nuts 12, Pina Colada Cream Cake with coconut cream mousse, fresh pineapple, mac nut sponge, pineapple chip garnish, raspberry and lilikoi sauces 11
Adult Beverages: Beer/Wine Cellar/Cocktails – Corkage Fee 25

Impressions: Good Life

Stroll across the Fairmont Orchid's beautiful grounds and you'll come to their oceanfront restaurant with its open-air atmosphere. Brown's Beach House is a traditional Kohala Coast favorite specializing in fresh fish and island inspired cuisine. Lunch is a casual affair with beach togs acceptable, but the code goes upscale in the evening. Guests can expect an experience reflecting the resort's notable standards. Those looking for romantic fine dining should do well here.

Big Island Dining

Hilo

Café 100 ✓

969 Kilauea Avenue
Hilo, HI 96720
808-935-8683
Web: None
Hours: B 6:45 AM-10:30 AM XSu
       LD 10:30 AM-7:30 PM XSuFr
       LD 10:30 AM-9:00 PM Fr
Cards: None
Dress: Casual
Style: Local $

Menu Sampler: Kids Menu Too

Breakfast:
Breakfast Plate, ham, bacon, Spam, Portuguese or Smokie sausage with 2 eggs and rice or toast 3.55, Sunriser of ham, egg, cheese on English muffin 2.75, Ham Omelet 3.75, Dad's Homemade Hotcakes 3.25, French Toast 2.75

Lunch/Dinner:
Plate Lunch: includes rice and mac salad, Beef Teriyaki Steak 6.45, Fried Chicken 5.25, Hamburger Steak 4.45, Mahimahi (or ahi in season) breaded, grilled or miso 6.75, Vegetable Dish (Hekka, Chop Sui, Etc.) 6.25, Hilo Boy Plate (Fried Chicken, Beef Teri, Stew) 6.95, Island Girl Plate (Breaded Shrimp, Beef Teri) 6.95, Lots of specials offered every day from 4.25 to 6.45
Loco Moco Family: Loco Moco 1.99, Double Loco 3.95, Chili Loco 2.95, Spam Loco 2.95, Kilauea Loco (with salad) 4.75, Super Loco (with salad) 4.75
Burgers & Sandwiches: Hamburger 1.75, Bacon Cheesy Girl 3.25, Garden Burger 3.55, Pastrami 2.95, Turkey 2.55, Teribeef 3.25, Mahimahi 3.55
Sides: Crispy Won Ton 2.95, French Fries 1.75, Soup of the Day 2.55
Sweets: Homemade Pie 2.25, Turnovers 1.95, Goody Good Sherbet .60
Adult Beverages: N/A

Impressions: Local Immersion

This family owned drive-in is a Hilo institution dating back to the late '40's. The original Café 100 location was down by the bay, but after it got washed away in a tsunami the owners decided to relocate on higher ground. The meals here are a solid representation of local comfort food. Customers line up at the window and place their orders before finding a seat at one of the covered picnic tables. Then it's time to experience the culinary world of the styrofoam tray. Prices are quite reasonable, portions are bountiful, and the place is neat as a pin. Those wanting to eat with the islanders can experience a real slice of Hilo at this establishment.

Big Island Dining

Hilo

Additional Location

Café Pesto ✓✓
308 Kamehameha Avenue
Hilo, HI 96720
808-969-6640
www.cafepesto.com
Hours: LD 11:00 AM-9:00 PM Su-Th
          LD 11:00 AM-10:00 PM Fr-Sa
Cards: AE DC DIS MC V
Dress: Casual
Style: Eclectic/Italian $$

Kawaihae Harbor Center
Kawaihae, HI 96743
808-882-1071

Menu Sampler: Kids Menu Too

Breakfast:
N/A

Lunch:
Appetizers: Smoked Salmon Pizzette rosemary gorgonzola, spinach $10.95
Salads: Thai Curry Shrimp over chilled fettuccine tossed with spinach, red onions & a red curry vinaigrette $12.95, Greek Pasta Salad $9.95
Calzones: Toscana, prosciutto ham, mushrooms and grainy Dijon mustard, Greek with spinach, feta cheese, olives $11.95 at lunch or $15.95 at dinner
Hot Sandwiches: Hakalau, warm Kalua turkey, wilted spinach, caramelized onions, Poha-mango chutney, garlic basted French bread $8.95

Dinner:
Appetizers: Asian Pacific Crab Cakes with honey-miso vinaigrette and pickled cucumber namasu $12.95, Focaccia with herbed goat cheese, Greek olive pesto, or rosemary gorgonzola $4.95, Sesame Crusted Big Island Goat Cheese $10.95
Gourmet Pizzas: 9" & 12" variety of traditional & gourmet $8.95 to $17.95
Entrées: Mango Glazed Chicken served w/caramelized mango chutney, garlic mashed potatoes and Pahoa corn relish $19.95, Coriander Grilled Tenderloin & Blackened Shrimp served w/garlic goat cheese mashed potatoes, honey buttered Manuka spinach, Hamakua mushroom jus $29.95, Stir Fry Beef & Veg $17.95
Adult Beverages: Beer/Wine Cellar/Cocktails – Corkage Fee $7.00

Impressions: Casually Chic

Visit the downtown district fronting Hilo Bay and you'll see Café Pesto with its old world bistro atmosphere. Here amidst the black and white tile flooring, high ceilings and café style chairs, the proprietors offer an eclectic menu appropriate to the ambiance. When ordering, it's like, "Wow!! Can I have one of these and two of those?" For patrons looking to spend time enjoying good company, Café Pesto offers lots of light bites and a full bar with an extensive wine and beer list.

Big Island Dining

Kohala

Coast Grille ✓✓✓
Hapuna Beach Prince Hotel
62-100 Kaunaoa Drive
Kohala Coast, HI 96743
808-880-1111
www.hapunabeachprincehotel.com
Hours: D 6:00-9:00 PM
Cards: AE JCB MC V
Dress: Resort Casual
Style: Pacific Rim/Seafood $$$

Menu Sampler: Kids Menu Too

Breakfast/Lunch:
N/A
Dinner:
Raw Bar: Top Quality Assortment of oysters, clams, mussels $Market Price
Appetizers: Manila Clam and Corn Chowder with roasted peppers $8, Shrimp Risotto, kabocha, sage pesto $18, Oven Roasted Scallops, pineapple jasmine rice, red curry glaze $12, Seared Hawaiian Ahi Summer Roll, green papaya salad, roasted peanut sauce $15, Sake Shoyu Steamed Manila Clams $16
Entrées: Grilled New York Steak, Shimegi Mushrooms, Maui onions, Waipio Fernshoot and wasabi peppercorn sauce $36, Pancetta Wrapped Filet Mignon, Kohala Vanilla Bean Demi-Glace & Lap-Xuong Bread pudding $38, Hawaiian Ono, fresh heart of palm salad, citrus tomato vinaigrette, tempura shrimp $35, Furikake Wasabi potato Crusted Salmon with shiso soy butter sauce $35
Desserts: Coconut Crème Dome $10, Mascarpone Amaretto Cheesecake Brulee $11, Chocolate Hazelnut Brioche Soufflé $10, Warm Valrhona Chocolate Cake $10, Coast Grille Dessert Sampler Plate $13, Trio of Sorbets $10
Adult Beverages: Beer/Wine Cellar/Cocktails – Corkage Fee $28

Impressions: Seafood Specialties

This spacious restaurant has an airy indoor seating area that complements the large outdoor lanai overlooking beautiful Hapuna Beach. A well-stocked raw bar offers a wide variety of fresh oysters and homemade poke that challenges patrons to forgo dinner for an evening of pupus. However, the upscale Pacific Rim menu will tempt you to your table. Expect to find interesting dishes with complex flavors across the menu. Seafood might be the focal point, but make sure to consider the beef dishes as well. Then there's always the dessert tray! The wait staff adds to the experience providing informative, efficient service. This is one resort dining room worth the effort of a special drive up the coast.

Big Island Dining

Waimea

Daniel Thiebaut ✓✓✓

65-1259 Kawaihae Road (Hwy 19)
Waimea, HI 96743
808-887-2200
www.danielthiebaut.com
Hours: Br 10:00 AM-1:30 PM Su
           D 3:30 PM-9:00 PM
Cards: AE DC DIS JCB MC V
Dress: Resort Casual
Style: French/Asian $$$

Menu Sampler: Kids Menu Too

Sunday Brunch:
Buffet of breakfast and dinner selections at a chef/owner level $23.50/$11.75
Dinner:
First Course: Lobster Bisque flavored with brandy and topped with cilantro coconut cream $7.50, Hilo Sweet Corn Crabcake with lemongrass-coconut lobster sauce, annato crème fraiche and mango salsa $9.50, Spicy Chicken Wonton with Big Island slaw and ginger soy mayonnaise dip $8.00
Entrées: Hunan Style Rack of Lamb with lamb jus, eggplant compote, Puna goat cheese and roasted potatoes $32.50, Grilled Bacon-Wrapped Tenderloin of Beef in Thai Curry - Balsamic Vinegar - Red Wine Sauce with Herb Spaetzle $28.00, Sautéed Macadamia Nut Chicken Breast with gingered mustard seed sauce, pickled pineapple and pave potatoes $22.50, Wok-Fried Sea Scallops with Asian Style Risotto and a Warm Coconut Crab Dressing $23.00, Mixed Seafood in an Orange Chili Garlic Sauce on Chow Fun Noodles $21.50, Chock In Style Stir-Fry Chicken in Peanut Sauce on Yaki Soba Noodles $21.50
Dessert: Fresh Papaya Millefeuille with vanilla sauce $6.50, Warm Strawberry Gratin with Tahitian vanilla ice cream $6.50, Chocolate & More $7.50
Prix Fixe: Three Course Prix Fixe $30.00 of first course, entrée & dessert
Adult Beverages: Beer/Wine Cellar/Cocktails – Corkage Fee $25.00

Impressions: Nouveau Plantation

Chef Daniel Thiebaut has transformed a quaint plantation general store into a wonderful setting for informal yet upscale dining. Note the counter and stools along one wall of the main room where the Parker Ranch paniolos used to sit and enjoy their beer. Some of their antique bottles are still on the shelves and even the old-fashioned fixtures remain in the bathrooms. The expansive menu uses fresh local ingredients and diverse techniques with pleasing results. Then the chef's classic talents are subtly applied to Asian dishes to enrich the exotic.

Big Island Dining

Kona

Don the Beachcomber ✓✓✓
Royal Kona Resort
75-5852 Alii Drive
Kailua-Kona, HI 96740
808-329-3111
www.hawaiihotels.com
Hours: B 6:30 AM-10:00 AM
          D 5:30 PM 9:00 PM XMoTu
Cards: AE DC DIS JCB MC V
Dress: Resort Casual
Style: Polynesian $$$

Menu Sampler: Kids Menu Too

Breakfast:
Two Eggs, home fries, toast and choice of ham, bacon or sausage 10.50, Kona Coast Benedict 13.50, Custard Toast 10.50, Mac Nut Cakes 6.50/8.50

Dinner:
Pupus: Kona Crab Cakes with roasted red bell pepper mango tartar sauce 12.95, Tropical Bries-brie rolled in shredded coconut, fried, with papaya and mango compote, mini-loaf 11.95, Seared Peppered Ahi w/pineapple-ginger sauce 10.95
Soups & Salads: Crab Scallop Chowder 4.00/6.00, Tiki Chicken Salad with special sesame seed dressing 11.95, Don's Salad de Corazon with lychee fruit, toasted macadamia nuts, zesty lemon-ginger dressing 10.95, House Salad 7.95
House Specialties: Prime Rib of Beef with au jus and creamy horseradish 21.95/25.95/31.95, The Hukilau of jumbo shrimp wrapped in pancetta, flame seared, served with passion fruit beurre blanc, coconut rice, vegetables 26.95
Entrées: Don's Famous Genghis Khan New York Steak Kabob 28.95, Mahi Mahi Mac Nut Crusted with tropical salsa, lomi lomi coconut rice, vegetables 29.95, Ahi Furikake with pineapple-ginger-coconut-wasabi sauce, sea salad, lychee fruit 29.95, Hawaiian Luau Plate 24.95, The Sword Fight 29.95
Adult Beverages: Beer/Wine/Cocktails

Impressions: Romantic Evening

Royal Kona Resort is undergoing a major retrofit to restore the property to its former glory. In keeping with that effort, management has cleared the decks in their waterfront dining room and created a new Don the Beachcomber. Dining enthusiasts who remember the Tiki restaurants of yore will feel right at home, and those born too late will finally get their chance. Early risers can relax over breakfast, but the main event takes place when the evening spectacle of torches and village lights dance on the water. Be sure to go early and take in the sunset.

Big Island Dining

Hilo

Don's Grill ✓✓
485 Hinano Street
Hilo, HI 96720
808-935-9099
Web: None
Hours: BLD 10:30 AM-8:30 PM Tu-Th, SaSu
        BLD 10:00 AM-10:00 PM Fr
Cards: AE MC V
Dress: Casual
Style: American/Island $

Menu Sampler: Kids Menu Too

Breakfast:
Ham & Cheese Omelet with rice or hashed browns and toast $6.25, Loco Moco an island original of a hamburger patty with a mound of rice, gravy and a fried egg $5.25, Double Loco Moco $7.95, Two Eggs with bacon, grilled fish, ham, Portuguese sausage, Spam, link sausage or corned beef hash $6.25, Sweetbread French Toast $4.95, Pancakes $4.25/$4.95, Steak & Eggs $10.95

Lunch/Dinner:
Entrées: served with hot vegetables, fresh roll and choice of rice, mashed potatoes or French fries, Rotisseried Chicken $7.95, Seafood Platter of breaded shrimp, breaded scallops and grilled filet of fish $10.50, Lasagna with hot vegetables & garlic bread $7.95, Grilled Teriyaki Beef $8.95, Grilled Pork Chops $9.50, Barbecue Ribs $8.95, Grilled Liver with onions & bacon $7.95
Burgers and Sandwiches: with choice of French fries, cole slaw or macaroni salad $5.25, Gardenburger $5.95, Reuben Sandwich $6.25, Patti Melt $6.25
Soups: Saimin $5.25, Won Ton Mein $6.95, Chili & Rice with cheese $5.25
Salads: Cobb Salad $8.25, Taco Salad $6.95, Chicken Caesar $7.50
Sweet Treats: Homemade Pie $2.95, Ala Mode $4.50, Cheesecake $3.25, With Strawberries $3.95, Milkshakes $3.50, Apple-Lumpia Ala Mode $4.25
Adult Beverages: Beer/Wine

Impressions: Hilo Homestyle

Not far from the airport there's a family dining place serving a solid menu with substantial portions at reasonable prices. Don's Grill is a favorite with the local crowd and those travelers fortunate enough to find it. This isn't fine dining, but the offerings are tasty and well prepared. The menu includes favorites from the plantation days as well as choices from a variety of cuisines. Think of Don's as an international comfort food station. The modern facility with its airy solarium seating brings that outdoor feeling so many find welcoming on a rainy Hilo day.

Big Island Dining

Kona

Drysdale's Two ✓✓
Keauhou Shopping Center
78-6831 Alii Drive
Kailua-Kona, HI 96740
808-322-0070
Web: None
Hours: LD 11:00 AM-11:00 PM
Cards: JCB MC V
Dress: Casual
Style: American $$

Menu Sampler:

Breakfast:
N/A

Lunch/Dinner:
Pupus: Chicken Fingers with hot sauce and French fries 8.85, Cheese Nachos & Jalapenos 8.35, Potato Skins 8.25, Shrimp Scampi with garlic toast 10.60
Burgers: Patty Melt on Grilled Rye 7.95, Baja Burger, melted cheese, green chilis 7.75, Aloha Burger, grilled pineapple slice, ham, cheese, BBQ sauce 8.15
Salads: Chef's Salad w/egg, ham, cheeses & turkey 10.95, Tuna Salad 10.60, Shrimp Salad w/1000 Island dressing 12.85, Cobb Salad w/crumbled blue cheese 11.60, Cajun Blackened Chicken Salad w/blue cheese dressing 10.75
Sandwiches: Fish Sandwich with fries 10.60, Italian Meatball Sandwich on a French roll with bell peppers & onions 8.60, Keauhou BLT with turkey 7.85
Plates: Tempura Fish & Chips 10.95, Oriental Chicken Stir-Fry with rice 13.35, Greek Gyros Sandwich with yogurt dill sauce 8.75, BBQ Pork Baby Back Ribs & onion rings 16.95, Sesame Pasta Sauté with chicken breast chunks, zucchini, snow peas, onions, linguini 12.35, Shrimp Basket with Fries and cocktail sauce 9.95, Prime Rib of Beef with French fries and au jus 11.60
Adult Beverages: Beer/Wine/Cocktails

Impressions: Sports Bar

There are times when a sports bar with a solid menu and an ocean view are just the ticket. If that mood strikes you, get in your car and take a ride to Drysdale's Two in the Keauhou Shopping Center. Casual dining is apropos at this friendly establishment, but the menu is quite broad and everyone should be able to find something to please. Check the daily specials board for the fresh catch choices and specialty dishes. If you just want to hang out grab a seat around the bar and relax with your favorite beverage while watching the live sports telecasts. There always seems to be a lively discussion going on among that opinionated crowd!

Big Island Dining

Hilo

Garden Snack Club ✓✓

80 Kilauea Avenue
Hilo, HI 96720
808-933-9664
Web: None
Hours: LD 11:00 AM-9:00 PM Tu-Th
         LD 11:00 AM- 9:30 PM FrSa
Cards: MC V
Dress: Casual
Style: Healthy Thai $

Menu Sampler:

Breakfast:
N/A
Lunch/Dinner:
Starters: Sticky Rice & Steamed Vegetables with Tina's Peanut Sauce $5, Summer Rolls, fresh vegetables wrapped in rice paper with shrimp or tofu and Tina's Special Sauce $5, Green Papaya or Cucumber Salad $6, Seafood Salad shrimp, squid, salmon and long rice tossed with Thai ingredients and hot and sour sauce served over organic greens $15, Mixed Green Salad with tofu $8
Soups: Small feeds two, large feeds four, served with tofu, add chicken $2, shrimp or fish $3, mixed seafood $4, Tom Yum $9/$12, Tom Kah $9/$12, Spicy Thai Basil $9/$12, Tina's Special Soup with opakapaka, lemongrass, spinach, enoki mushrooms, green onions and cherry tomato $15
Entrées: Garlic Shrimp, Salmon, Curry Fish or Shrimp Sandwich with fresh organic greens, cucumber, tomato and pineapple $7, Thai Pizza with spinach, Thai basil, pineapple, onion, red curry, coconut milk, cheddar cheese layered between two spinach tortillas with tofu $10, shrimp $12, seafood or fish $15, Opakapaka with black bean sauce, garlic, ginger, brown and green onion $15, Curry Pineapple Stir-fry with tofu $10, shrimp $12, seafood or fish $15, Salmon with asparagus and Thai hot sauce $18, Jasmine or Sticky Rice $2
Adult Beverages: BYOB

Impressions: Spicy Organic

Here's an interesting alternative when you're thinking alternative! Their name might not convey an accurate impression, but the menu gets right to the point. This is a healthy dining establishment that combines Thai recipes, spices, and flavors with organic ingredients. The food is pleasant to the taste, good for the body and easy on the pocketbook. That's a pretty hard combination to beat! A short stroll up the quiet end of Kilauea Avenue will take you to this storefront.

Kona

Harbor House ✓✓
Honokohau Harbor
74-425 Kealakehe Parkway
Kailua-Kona, HI 96740
808-326-4166
Web: None
Hours: LD 11:00 AM-6:45 PM Mo-Sa
          LD 11:00 AM-6:00 PM Su
Cards: AE MC V
Dress: Casual
Style: American Casual $

Menu Sampler: Kids Menu Too

Breakfast:
N/A
Lunch/Dinner:
Pupus: Hawaiian Poke, raw fish Hawaiian style $8.95, Smoked Pork Sautéed with Onion $6.50, Seafood Spring Rolls $6.25, Takoyaki-Octopus Puff $5.25, French Fries $3.75, Garden Salad with Teriyaki Chicken $9.00, Clam Chowder $3.50/$4.75, Edamame $2.75, Chicken Strips $6.75, Onion Rings $5.75
Specials: Fish & Chips w/fries $9.95, Calamari & Chips $8.95, Fried Chicken & Chips $9.00, Cup of Chili $4.25, Chili & Rice $6.25, Saimin noodle soup $4.95
Burgers & Sandwiches: all come with fries, Hamburger $6.95, Teriyaki Burger $7.25, Chili Burger $8.50, Grilled Fresh Fish Sandwich $9.75, Garden Burger $7.00, Grilled Cheese Sandwich $5.00, Philly Cheese Steak Sandwich w/cheese & grilled onions on French bread $8.95, Jumbo Hot Dog $6.25, Jumbo Chili Dog $7.75, Bacon, Lettuce, Tomato Sandwich $6.25, Ham Hoagie $6.75
Entrées: all come with rice, macaroni salad & small green salad, Catch of the Day $10.50, Fried Chicken Platter $9.75, Vegetable Stirfry $8.50, w/fish $9.75
Dessert: Vanilla Ice Cream $2.75, Root Beer, Coke & Iced Coffee Floats $4.75
Adult Beverages: Beer/Wine

Impressions: Marina Friendly

When told what we do West Hawaii types often ask, "Have you tried the Harbor House?" immediately followed by, "They've got a great mug of iced-cold beer!" With a recommendation like that we had no choice but to troop over to the small boat marina and give it a try. The verdict is in – yes they do have a great mug of beer, and better yet they offer an affordable menu reminiscent of the tavern food served before automatic frybots replaced cooks. There's something for everyone as fresh-off-the-boat fish plates and burger baskets appear next to local favorites.

Big Island Dining

Waimea

Hawaiian Style Café ✓
64-1290 Kawaihae Road (Hwy 19)
Waimea, HI 96743
808-885-4295
Web: None
Hours: BL 7:00 AM-1:30 PM Mo-Sa
B 7:00 AM-12:00 PM Su
Cards: None
Dress: Casual
Style: Hawaiian/American/Regional $

Menu Sampler: Kids Menu Too

Breakfast:
Two Eggs, choice of meat, rice or hash browns and toast or pancakes $6.95,
Three Egg Omelette, meat, mushroom, onion and cheese, rice or hash browns
and pancake or toast $7.25, Loco Moco $7.25, Two Pancakes $4.50, Sweet
Bread French Toast $5.50, Corned Beef Hash, Two Eggs & Fried Rice $7.25,
Pork Chop & Eggs $8.95. Steak & Eggs $9.25, Lite Breakfast $5.50

Lunch:
Burgers and Sandwiches: Teri Burger Single $6.25/Double $7.25, Cheese
Burger $6.25/$7.50, BLT with Maui chips and potato-mac salad $7.25,
Clubhouse $7.75, Tuna $6.50, Fries $2.75, Maui Potato Chips $1.50,
Plate Lunches: all served with rice and potato-mac salad, Korean Chicken fried
then dipped in our homemade sweet yet spicy Korean marinade $7.95, Kalbi
Ribs grilled with a sweet sesame shoyu flavor $8.95, Pork Chops covered with
grilled onions, brown gravy $8.95, Honey Stung Fried Chicken $7.50, Chicken
Cutlet $7.50, 8 oz Striploin Steak grilled medium or as specified $9.25
Keiki Breakfast $3.25, **Keiki Lunch** $3.50, **Split Charge** $2.00
Adult Beverages: N/A
Dinner:
N/A

Impressions: Prodigious Platters

This was once your typical small town café where everybody knew one another,
and the proprietor struggled to balance the books at the end of each month. That
era closed suddenly when the media "discovered" the Hawaiian Style Café. Now
you might have to wait for a table, but it's worthwhile as the same cooks prepare
mountains of local comfort food guaranteed to satisfy a teenager's appetite. That
and the consistently affordable prices make it an automatic recommendation. Go
early as they close when the food runs out. The Hawaiians call this, "Pau Hana!"

Big Island Dining

Hilo

Hilo Bay Café ✓✓✓
Waiakea Center
315 Maka'ala Street
Hilo, HI 96720
808-935-4939
www.hilobaycafe.com

Hours: L 11:00 AM-5:00 PM Mo-Sa
          D 5:00 PM-9:00 PM
Cards: AE DC DIS MC V
Dress: Resort Casual
Style: American/European/Asian $$

Menu Sampler:
Kids Menu Too

Breakfast:
N/A

Lunch:
Appetizers: Ahi Poke with sweet potato chips 10, Guinness onion rings 8
Salads: Blackened Ahi Caesar with Kekela organic baby romaine lettuce and parmesan chips 11, Crab Cakes with Asian sesame dressing 12
Sandwiches: all come served with choice of garlic fries, jicama slaw or rice, Grilled Portobello mushroom with tomatoes, dill havarti, horseradish cream 9
Entrées: Pork BBQ Ribs, sweet corn, garlic fries 12, Flaky Crust Pot Pie with savory vegetables, served with mixed greens 9, Fresh Catch Fish & Chips 13

Dinner:
Appetizers: Parmesan Baked Artichoke Dip 8, Ahi Carpaccio with truffle oil and aioli 10, Cumin Blue Prawn, Scallop and Risotto Cake 12
Salads: Grilled Free Range Chicken Breast with Hamakua Springs heirloom tomatoes, gorgonzola cheese and tabasco onions 10
Entrées: Macadamia Nut Praline Seared Scallops with smoked bacon and angel hair pasta 18, Grilled Kulana New York Strip Steak with brown butter whipped potatoes, asparagus and Hawaiian vanilla bordelaise 27
Adult Beverages: Beer/Wine Cellar/Cocktails – Corkage Fee 25

Impressions:
Classy Storefront

Hilo has been characterized as a sleepy little provincial backwater. Maybe that's why we like it so much! Well friends, Hilo is growing up. We've seen no better example of the transition in dining than the Hilo Bay Café. A few years ago this strip mall location might have been serving plate lunch. Instead, an avant dining venue has moved in and an upscale crowd has appeared. The cuisine doesn't fall into the usual categories. Rather, it's innovative with a personality all of its own.

Kona

Huggo's ✓✓
75-5828 Kahakai Road
Kailua-Kona, HI 96740
808-329-1493
www.huggos.com
Hours: L 11:30 AM-2:30 PM Mo-Fr
        D 5:30 PM-10:00 PM
Cards: AE DC DIS JCB MC V
Dress: Casual
Style: American/Eclectic $$

Menu Sampler: Kids Menu Too

Breakfast:
N/A

Lunch:
All sandwiches and burgers are served with choice of pineapple cole slaw, fries, rice and sliced tomatoes. Classic Huggo Burger with sautéed onions, mushrooms and choice of cheddar or swiss $11.95, Mac Nut Chicken Katsu Plate Lunch with rice $12.95, Chinese Chicken Salad with sesame vinaigrette $11.95, Fresh Catch broiled, grilled, sautéed or blackened $Mkt

Dinner:
Appetizers: Fish Trap Shrimp in a net of fried, shredded phyllo dough with sweet chili dipping sauce $14.95, Garlic Bread Parmesan $6.95, Poke $Mkt
Soups & Salads: Spinach Salad with goat cheese and orange segments $10.95, Seafood Chowder $5.95/$7.95, Classic Caesar $8.95/$10.95, Green Salad $8.95
Entrées: Char-broiled NY Steak, coriander rub, chipotle demi-glace, avocado salsa, garlic mashed potatoes, asparagus $34.95, Crab Crusted Ono with mozzarella and parmesan cheese, mango vinaigrette, rice, vegetables $32.95, Lilikoi Miso Ahi, wasabi macadamia nut mashed potatoes, vegetables $34.95, Seafood Linguine in a sherry cream sauce $29.95, Lemon Cashew Seafood Stirfry, snow peas, onions, cashews in a lemon sherry sauce, brown rice $28.95, Ginger Orange Chicken, rice, vegetables $26.95
Adult Beverages: Beer/Wine Cellar/Cocktails – Corkage Fee $10.00-$15.00

Impressions: Wavefront Dining

This rocky stretch of waterfront comes in several incarnations. First, there's Huggo's which is a casual seaside dining spot. Then a step away you'll find Huggo's On The Rocks, which can best be described as a watering hole and place to see and be seen. Finally, around dawn Java On The Rock shows up serving Kona coffee and pastries to those bleary-eyed denizens of the night.

Big Island Dining

Waimea

Huli Sue's Barbecue & Grill ✓✓
64-957 Mamalahoa Hwy (Hwy 19)
Waimea, HI 96743
808-885-6268
www.hulisues.com
Hours: L 11:30 AM-5:00 PM
              D 5:00 PM-8:30 PM
Cards: AE DC DIS JCB MC V
Dress: Casual
Style: Barbecue $$

Menu Sampler: Kids Menu Too

Breakfast:
N/A
Lunch:
Hearty Dishes: available all day, Coconut Curry - Vegetable $12, Chicken $14, Fish $16, Black Bean Chili $10, Smoked Meat Sandwiches w/slaw & fries $10
BBQ: all served with fries, slaw and soda, Pork Roast $15, Pork Ribs $17, Half Free Range Chicken $15, Lamb Leg $16, Beef Brisket $15, Beef Short Ribs $18
Dinner:
Pupus: Margarita Poke with corn, onions, chilis, cilantro and cornnuts $10, Mama's Famous Thai Style Caesar Salad with Black Pepper Bacon $10
Plates: include a bowl of greens or a trip to the salad bar, 12 Oz Strip Steak with purple basil, chimmichuri on garlic mash $24, Grilled 8 oz Pork Chop w/bourbon-brown sugar on corn pudding $17, Grilled Island Fish with hot & sour eggplant relish and tsuyu drizzle on rice $23, Big Burger with fries $12
Sauces: Paniolo Chipotle-Southwestern, Mandarin Honey Mojo-Caribbean, Chili Water, Pineapple & Sugar Cane and Crackseed-Hawaiian
Sides: Grilled Pineapple Rings, Beer Battered Onion Rings, Black Beans, Rice, Corn Pudding, Ranch Dill Slaw, Mac Salad and Homemade French Fries $4 ea
Adult Beverages: Beer/Wine

Impressions: Country Roadhouse

Huli Sue's menu makes an intriguing statement about those who operate this establishment. On one hand you're offered classic barbequed meats, but then garlic mash appears as a side dish. Before you know it the Mexican influence weighs in along with a host of spicy sauces from various corners of the globe. It's all great fun giving guests an opportunity to experiment with flavors they might not ordinarily encounter. Don't let the long tables and benches confuse you, this Waimea country barbeque is miles away from the Mississippi River.

Big Island Dining

Kohala

Imari ✓✓
Hilton Waikoloa Village
425 Waikoloa Beach Drive
Waikoloa, HI 96738
808-886-1234
www.HiltonWaikoloaVillage.com
Hours: D 5:30 PM-9:30 PM
Cards: AE DIS JCB MC V
Dress: Evening Aloha
Style: Japanese Fusion $$$$

Menu Sampler: Kids Menu Too

Breakfast/Lunch:
N/A
Dinner:
Appetizers, Soups, Salads: Edamame 7, Tempura Moriawase with shrimp and assorted vegetables 16, Imari Salad with Imari Dressing 11, Sautéed Foie Gras and Unagi with mirin balsamic glaze over rice cake 25, New Wave Sashimi 19
Entrées: Imari Miso Butterfish 28, Keahole Lobster poached in sake and Ichiban dashi with leek, watercress and daikon oroshi 55, Teriyaki Chicken Breast with island shiitake mushrooms and lemon-lime teriyaki sauce 30
Specialty Dinners: Shabu Shabu of thin sliced American raised Kobe Beef and vegetables in sukiyaki sauce or kombu broth, steamed rice, tsukemono & green tea ice cream 53 per person, two person minimum
Sashimi and Sushi: Maguro Sashimi of fresh ahi served with wasabi and soy sauce 18, California Roll of crab, avocado & cucumber 14, Spider Roll 18
Teppanyaki: with assorted vegetables, Imari salad, Edamame, rice, miso soup and tsukemono, Filet Mignon 47, Shrimp and Jumbo Scallops 46, Steak and Shrimp 54, Catch of the Day 44, Lobster Tail 65, Breast of Chicken 39, Vegetarian Dinner 34, Steak and Lobster 63, New York Steak 45
Adult Beverages: Beer/Wine/Cocktails – Corkage Fee 33

Impressions: Everything Japanese

Upon entering Imari you will be immersed in all things Japanese. Kimono clad waitresses and attendants seat and serve you from a choice of traditional dining styles. Dinner guests can choose from teppanyaki table, sushi bar, tatami room, and conventional table seating. Chef Atsumi is classically trained and employs the freshest of ingredients to create his healthy selections. Meanwhile the clean contemporary lines and generous use of wood conveys the decor of Japan. You won't find a better example of architectural correctness in the neighbor islands.

Big Island Dining

Kona

Island Lava Java Bistro & Grill ✓✓
Alii Sunset Plaza
75-5799 Alii Drive
Kailua-Kona, HI 96740
808-327-2161
www.islandlavajavakona.com
Hours: B 6:30 AM-11:30 AM
        L 11:30 AM-4:30 PM
        D 4:30 PM-9:30 PM
Cards: AE DIS JCB MC V
Dress: Casual
Style: Coffee/Bistro $$

Menu Items: Kids Menu Too

Breakfast:
Bagelwich $4.50, Island Eggs Benedict with ham $11.50, with smoked salmon or grilled shrimp $14.00, Big Kahuna Steak and Eggs $12.95, Waffles with bacon or sausage $7.95, Short Stack of Pancakes, bacon or sausage $7.95, Ham, egg and cheese croissant $5.25, Island Bagel & Lox $8.50, Cup of Fruit $3.95

Lunch:
Kohala Steak Sandwich with caramelized onions, shiitake mushrooms, arugula and horseradish aioli, fries or salad $13.95, Sunset Rueben Sandwich with fries or salad $9.50, Fresh Fish Tacos with black beans and salad $12.95, Shawn's Spinach Salad $9.95, Delicatessen Sandwiches $8.50 to $9.75

Dinner:
Paniolo New York Steak with jalapeno gorgonzola butter, grilled vegetables and onion rings $26.95, Grilled Fresh Fish with tropical salsa, grilled vegetables and black beans Mkt Price, Butternut Squash & Rosemary Lasagne w/salad $11.95, Portobello Mushroom Sandwich w/gorgonzola & roasted red pepper vinaigrette $11.95, Captain Cook's Crab Salad Sandwich on focaccia $9.95, Caesar Salad $8.95, add grilled shrimp or grilled steak slices $5.50, Grilled Fresh Fish Tacos & salad $10.95, Children's Plates $2.85 to $4.25

Adult Beverages: N/A

Impressions: Seaside Gourmet

Island Lava Java has crossed over from the world of coffeehouses to that of full service restaurants offering three meals a day. This is not a half-hearted attempt. Their new menus are quite extensive. We like the variety of portions and prices that make this an easy choice regardless of a party's appetite. As an added plus, their location provides a front row seat to the people-watching along Alii Drive.

Big Island Dining

Kona

Jackie Rey's Ohana Grill ✓✓
75-5995 Kuakini Highway
Kailua-Kona, HI 96740
808-327-0209
Web: None
Hours: L 11:00 AM-2:00 PM Mo-Fr
        D 5:00 PM-9:00 PM
Cards: AE DIS MC V
Dress: Casual
Style: Island $$$

Menu Sampler: Kids Menu Too

Breakfast:
N/A
Lunch:
Ohana Cobb with sesame soy dressing 6.95/8.95, Sizzlin' Sweet & Sour Shrimp
with pineapple, onions, steamed rice, side salad 13.95, BBQ Pork Sandwich
with choice of curly fries, tossed salad or pineapple yogurt slaw 9.95, Mac Nut
Basil Chicken Sandwich with fries or salad, tomatoes, avocado, provolone 8.50,
Blackened Salmon Plate, pineapple relish, rice and side salad 9.50
Dinner:
Pupus: Shrimp wontons with crab stuffing, sesame lime mayo 8.95, Beer
Battered Fresh Catch, miso sake sauce, wasabi drizzle 9.95, Soup 5.95
Salads: Club Med Salad with hummus, grilled garlic pita bread, Tabouleh,
greens, cucumbers, tomatoes, feta, calamata olives, basil pesto vinaigrette 12.95
Entrées: Seared Wasabi Ahi w/crispy noodles, Asian veg, ginger yaki glaze,
scallion oil 25.95, Seared NY Steak, rosemary mac-nut onion rings, mashers,
green peppercorns 31.95, Grilled Jumbo Scallops, lobster-crab Newburg sauce,
garlic mash 25.95, Chicken Marsala Fettuccini, seared breast, light garlic cream,
mushrooms & onions 19.95, Grilled Fresh Catch, jasmine rice, grilled veg 23.95
Adult Beverages: Beer/ Wine/Cocktails

Impressions: Easy Call

We're never quite sure what we're going to order when we stop at Jackie Rey's,
but we are sure we'll enjoy it. The menu meanders about touching on a number
of cuisines and approaches so take your pick. Escaping the predictable becomes
easy at this out-of-the-way casual dining venue. It's simple enough to find, and
once you're there take some time to enjoy the evening. The bartender knows to
pour a good drink, and nobody is in a hurry to turn the tables. Fresh fish always
ranks high on the agenda so be sure to ask what the day boat trollers brought in.

Big Island Dining

Waimea

Jade Palace Chinese Restaurant ✓✓
Waimea Shopping Center
65-1158 Mamalahoa Hwy (Hwy 19)
Waimea, HI 96743
808-887-1788
Web: None
Hours: LD 10:30 AM-9:00 PM
Cards: AE MC V
Dress: Casual
Style: Chinese $$

Menu Sampler:

Breakfast:
N/A

Lunch/Dinner:
Appetizers: Char Siu $7.95, Crispy Won Ton $4.95, Crab Rangoon $5.95, Sampler Platter $11.95, Spring Roll $4.95, Deep Fried Butterfly Prawns $8.95
Soups: Hot & Sour Soup $8.95, Won Ton Soup $8.95, Chicken Corn $8.95, Abalone with Black Mushroom Soup $9.95, Dried Scallop Soup $12.95
Entrées: Shrimp with Asparagus $12.95, Shrimp Two Flavor $18.95, Fish Filet with seasonal greens $11.95, Kung Po Chicken $9.95, Orange Chicken $9.95, Mu Shu Pork $9.95, Mongolian Beef $8.95, Egg Fu Yong $7.95, Tofu with assorted mushroom $8.95, Stir Fried Assorted Vegetable with Garlic $7.95, Minced Chicken with Lettuce Wrapped $14.95, Moo Goo Gai Pan $9.95
Sizzling Platter: Beef Tenderloin with Black Pepper Sauce $14.95, Boneless Chicken with Black Bean Sauce $12.95, Seafood Combination $14.95
Rice and Noodle: Shredded Pork Chow Mein $8.95, Yang Chow Fried Rice $9.95, Duck Noodle Soup $11.95, Char Siu Saimin $7.95, Wor Mein $8.95
House Specialty: Shrimp with Honey Glaze Walnuts $13.95, Twice Cook Pork $9.95, Dragon & Phoenix Sizzling Platter $13.95, Capital Pork Ribs $9.95
Adult Beverages: Beer/Wine

Impressions: Finer Service

Back in the plantation days Chinese immigrants left the neighbor islands as soon as they could for Honolulu and opportunity. This process seems to have reversed itself as Chinese entrepreneurs from Honolulu recently opened their restaurant in Waimea. This comes as a great improvement for diners who prefer the variety of provincial cuisines available on Oahu but not the Big Island. It's all done with a bit more flare than is usually found in locally influenced ethnic eateries. Clothed tables and proper service raise the bar as the kitchen prepares exciting new tastes.

Big Island Dining

Kona

Jameson's By The Sea ✓✓
Magic Sands Beach
77-6452 Alii Drive
Kailua-Kona, HI 96740
808-329-3195
www.jamesonshawaii.com
Hours: L 11:00 AM-2:00 PM Mo-Fr
       D 5:00 PM-8:30 PM
Cards: AE MC V
Dress: Casual
Style: Seafood $$

Menu Sampler: Kids Menu Too

Breakfast:
N/A
Lunch:
Appetizers: Salmon Pâté $12.95, Fried Calamari $12.95, Sashimi $17.95
Burgers & Sandwiches: Cheeseburger $9.95, Grilled Crab & Shrimp $14.95, Reuben $12.95, Deep Fried Calamari Steak Sandwich $14.95
Salads/Entrées: Curried Chicken Salad $14.95, Thai Chicken Salad $14.95, Chicken or Shrimp Caesar Salad $14.95, Jameson's Crab Louie $20.95, Seafood Quiche with choice of salads $12.95, Ono $16.95, Grilled Crab & Shrimp on sourdough $13.95, Grilled Reuben on light rye $12.95, Teriyaki Steak 15.95
Dinner:
Appetizers: Sashimi $17.95, Crab Stuffed Mushrooms $12.95, Fried Calamari $12.95, Chilled Seafood Platter $20.95, Sautéed Mushrooms $7.95
Entrées: Opakapaka prepared five ways $Market Price usually $32.00-$38.00, Baked Stuffed Shrimp with crabmeat, cheese and hollandaise $24.95, Seafood Diablo $23.95, Shrimp Curry with mango chutney $23.95, New York Steak $28.95, Filet Mignon with béarnaise $32.95, Shrimp Scampi on linguini $23.95
Adult Beverages: Beer/Wine Cellar/Cocktails – Corkage Fee $10.00

Impressions: Seaside Charmer

Jameson's typifies what visitors imagine when they think of Hawaii dining. This truly waterfront restaurant is located on the lower floor of a condo building next to Magic Sands Beach. Diners can choose from indoor or outdoor seating. Both come with lovely sunset views. Make no mistake, seafood preparations are king on this menu. Landlubbers might be happier elsewhere. After dinner sample one of the homemade chiffon pies. The shortbread crusts and island inspired fillings are delightful. If you enjoy ocean air dining this might be just what you're after.

Big Island Dining

Kohala

Kamuela Provision Company ✓✓
Hilton Waikoloa Village
69-425 Waikoloa Beach Drive
Waikoloa, HI 96738
808-886-1234
www.HiltonWaikoloaVillage.com
Hours: D 5:30 PM-9:30 PM
Cards: AE DIS JCB MC V
Dress: Resort Casual
Style: Hawaii Regional Cuisine $$$

Menu Sampler: Kids Menu Too

Breakfast/Lunch:
N/A
Dinner:
Appetizers: Volcano Charred Hawaiian Ahi with three bean rice and ponzu sauce 17, Golden Fried Macadamia Nut Shrimp with passion orange chili dipping sauce 17, Roasted Poblano Crab-Relleno 16, KPC Limu Poke 16
Soup & Salad: Tahitian Curried Creamy Crab Soup 11, Spinach Salad with hard-boiled egg, marinated mushrooms and warm bacon dressing 11
Specialties: Mauka and Makai filet of beef served on garlic mashed potatoes and sautéed spinach topped w/tempura lobster and seared foie gras 55, Guava BBQ Grilled Free Range Bird 29, Dijon Mustard, Herbed Rack of Lamb 40
Seafood: Pacific Salmon Brule 32, Macadamia Nut Crusted Snapper 36, Grilled, Sautéed or Blackened Fresh Fish of the Day (two selections daily) 36
Signature Steaks: with choice of sauces - green peppercorn, gorgonzola butter, sweet chili or merlot, 8 oz Grilled Medallions of Beef 30, 18 oz Porterhouse 49, 7 oz Grilled Filet Mignon 41, 12 oz Rib Eye Steak aged for 28 days 44
Desserts: KPC S'Mores 13, Warm Flourless Chocolate Lava Cake 13, KPC Original Coconut Crème Brulee 13, Molokai Lime Pie 11, Mud Pie 12
Adult Beverages: Beer/Wine Cellar/Cocktails

Impressions: Pacific Potpourri

Fusion cuisine using local ingredients was once a culinary novelty but became a mainstay when fine dining restaurateurs discovered the potential. Early on chefs across Hawaii began experimenting with new combinations employing existing methods and flavors. Kamuela Provision Company's table was designed around this approach. Here guests can expect to have complexity of preparation used to expose great tastes superior to the sum of the parts. Skillful presentation, proper service and an upscale setting complete the experience at this longtime standard.

Big Island Dining

Kona

Kanaka Kava √
Coconut Grove Marketplace
75-5803 Alii Drive
Kailua-Kona, HI 96740
808-327-1660
www.kanakakava .com
Hours: LD 10:00 AM-10:00 PM Su-We
       LD 10:00 AM-11:00 PM Th-Sa
Cards: None
Dress: Casual
Style: Island $$

Menu Sampler:

Breakfast:
N/A

Lunch/Dinner:
Ala Carte: Kalua Pork $5, Poke (Raw Fish) $5, Squid Luau $5, Opihi $5, Poi $4, Mixed Vegetables $5, Sweet Potato $4, Taro steamed with coconut milk $4, Garlic Bread $3, Ulu (when available) $4, Haupia/Sweet Potato Pie $4

Plates: all plates come with two ala Carte items, Fresh Fish $16, Chicken/Tofu Plate $13, Lau lau Plate $14, Seafood Plate-scallops, shrimp, fish $16, Pupu Platter-pork, sweet potato, poke, taro or ulu, poi, squid luau $16

Kava Menu: Fresh Kava (with or without juice) $5, Kavalada - blended kava drink with coconut milk and pineapple juice $6, Gingerade $5, Coconut Water $3, Fruit Juice $1, Bottled Water $1, Noni Juice (2oz) $2

Adult Beverages: Kava should never be consumed with alcohol

Impressions: Awa Bar

Kanaka Kava is not your ordinary everyday eatery. This is a kava bar. If you're not familiar with kava bars, we should probably start at the beginning. Kava is an adult beverage made from the root of the intoxicating pepper. Although non-alcoholic, kava has a definite kick to it hence the reason it is served at kava bars. The kava ritual begins in the late afternoon when an eclectic assembly of guests begins consuming small bowls of this interesting beverage followed by relaxing, eating and visiting. This is happy hour Polynesian style and is recommended for adventurous travelers. Enjoy the experience, but avoid driving home afterwards.

Kona

Ke'ei Café at Hokukano ✓✓✓

79-7511 Mamalahoa Hwy (Hwy 11)
Kealakekua, HI 96750
808-322-9992
Web: None
Hours: L 11:00 AM-2:00 PM Tu-Fr
         D 5:00 PM-9:00 PM Tu-Sa
Cards: None
Dress: Resort Casual
Style: Pacific Rim $$$

Menu Sampler: Small Plates Too

Breakfast:
N/A
Lunch:
Chilled Gazpacho with focaccia bread bowl 4.95, Wilted Spinach Salad, parmesan, cashews, Mandarin orange segments, olives 8.95, Mushroom Fettucini with onions, arugula, garlic, parmesan, tomatoes, basil pesto 11.95, Soba Noodles with choice of sesame crusted fresh fish, tofu or chicken with Oriental vegetables, crispy won ton and sesame vinaigrette 10.95, Grilled Eggplant Sandwich with Swiss cheese, tomatoes and hummus aioli 9.95
Dinner:
Starters: Chef Zeze's Coconut Shrimp Cake of shrimp and brown rice, coated with shredded coconut, pan seared then finished in the oven 6.95, Peanut Miso Salad with grated green papaya slivers on a bed of fresh mixed greens 5.95
Entrées: Nightly Fresh Catch with house famous Ke'ei Café Thai Curry Sauce or Pan Seared with caramelized onions & lemon caper butter sauce 20.95, Two Spicy Fajitas of chicken or tofu in a black bean, onion & pepper stir fry with lettuce, salsa, avocados & sour cream, wrapped in soft tortillas 13.95, Roasted Pork Chops with peppercorn gravy or sliced pineapple glaze 15.95
Adult Beverages: Beer/Wine Cellar/Cocktails – Corkage Fee 9.00

Impressions: Stylish Hideaway

A few miles south of Kailua-Kona you'll find one of West Hawaii's favorite hot spots. Those in pursuit of unique experiences would do well to give it a try. This family owned establishment prides itself in serving creative Pacific Rim cuisine. The chef takes a bold approach with flavoring which comes as no surprise when you consider the owners' Brazilian background. If you have a penchant for great panoramic views you might want to consider scheduling lunch or doing an early dinner. Parking is easily accessed by driving up the ramp alongside the building.

Kona

Additional Location

Kenichi Pacific ✓✓✓
Keauhou Shopping Center
78-6831 Alii Drive
Kailua-Kona, HI 96740
808-322-6400
Web: None
Hours: D 5:00 PM-9:00 PM XMo
Cards: AE MC V
Dress: Resort Casual
Style: Japanese/Pacific Rim $$$

Additional Location

The Shops at Mauna Lani
68-1330 Mauna Lani Dr
Kohala Coast, HI 96743
808-881-1515

Menu Sampler:

Small Plates Too

Breakfast/Lunch:
N/A

Dinner:

Starters: Dynamite Shrimp of tempura shrimp baked with smelt aioli and teriyaki sauce 6, Total Raw & Local of organic vegetables, sprouted grains and dehydrated buckwheat with a miso Caesar 10, Hijiki Rice with Hijiki seaweed 3

Appetizers: Fresh Lobster Summer Rolls wrapped with mint, cilantro, basil, pineapple and two dipping sauces 16, Tenderloin Carpaccio with ponzu 18

Entrées: Kenichi's Duck Confit of Chinese, five spice cured duck leg with celeriac puree, Alii mushrooms, pea tendrils, red pepper coulis and balsamic reduction 28, Bamboo Salmon with mixed vegetables and cranberry miso sauce 27, Macadamia Crusted Lamb, Colorado lamb chops coated with pan toasted macadamia nuts, accompanied by taro "risotto" & sweet black vinegar gastrique 42, Ono Tataki, grilled rare w/mashed yams, green beans, oyster mushrooms & a ponzu emulsion 29, Grilled Organic New York Steak, mashed yams & grilled bok choy, prepared teriyaki, wasabi oroshi ponzu or mushroom demi 37

Tempura: (2-3 pieces per order) asparagus 4, pumpkin 3, shrimp 7, tofu 3

Sushi: (6 pieces per order) Tuna Roll 6.50, Fresh Water Eel Roll 8.00

Sashimi: Toro $Mkt, Yellowtail 18.50, Salmon 17.00, Halibut 17.00

Adult Beverages: Beer/Wine Cellar/Cocktails – Corkage Fee 15

Impressions:

Contemporary Classic

Welcome to the West Side's newest foodie magnet. This is not a menu for timid tastes. Guests begin with traditional sushi before moving on to some of the most innovative contemporary Pacific Rim cuisine found in Hawaii. The preparations and ingredients lean toward high-end giving the kitchen a "Sky's the limit" view when designing their menu. Expect Japanese influences to appear regularly in all that they offer. Sister restaurants in Austin and Aspen add cachet and credibility.

Big Island Dining

Hilo

Ken's House of Pancakes ✓✓
1730 Kamehameha Avenue
Hilo, HI 96720
808-935-8711
Web: None
Hours: BLD 24/7
Cards: AE DC DIS JCB MC V
Dress: Casual
Style: American/Island $

Menu Sampler: Kids Menu Too

Breakfast/Lunch/Dinner:
The entire menu is available 24 hours a day seven days a week. Macadamia Nut Waffles $6.95, Fresh Banana Pancakes $6.10, Eggs Benedict $8.85, Crab Cakes Benedict $9.95, Loco Moco $5.95, Saimin $6.25, 23 Famous Omelette Choices, Florentine Omelet with spinach and sour cream, hashed browns or white or brown rice and toast or pancakes $9.35, Homemade muffin with honey butter $1.00, Burgers $6.85/$9.75 with fries or salad, BBQ Kalua Pig Sandwich on a grilled hoagie bun $8.45, Broiled Mahi Mahi Sandwich with cottage cheese or a green salad $8.95, Hot Turkey Sandwich with mashed potatoes and gravy $9.95, Dinner entrees come with mac salad, choice of rice, fries or mashed potatoes. Broiled Teriyaki Chicken $9.45, Grilled Pork Chops $9.95, Honey Stung Chicken $9.75, Liver Lovers with grilled onions, bacon and gravy $9.75, Kalbi Ribs with Kim Chee $13.95, Vegetarian BLT $8.65, Oxtail Stew $11.95, Tuesday after 3 PM is all-you-can-eat taco night. Wednesday after 3 PM is Paniolo Night with a Prime Rib special. Thursday after 3 PM is Hawaiian Plate and local specialty night. Sunday after 3 PM is all-you-can-eat spaghetti night.
Desserts: Milk Shakes $3.75, Ice Cream Floats $3.50, Sundaes of strawberry, blueberry, chocolate, lilikoi & coconut $2.10 to $4.25, Sweet Potato Pie with haupia topping $3.25, Macadamia Nut Pie $2.45, Fresh Papaya $1.85
Adult Beverages: N/A

Impressions: Comfort Zone

This old Hilo standard serves an extensive mainland and island menu in a coffee shop/diner setting. Ken's is especially convenient being located just to the north of the airport entrance. Long distance travelers seem to suffer from maladjusted body clocks, which is where Ken's really shines. You're talking 24/7 service all year long which is unheard of in the neighbor islands. Guests can expect to find solid fare served at reasonable prices in this clean, well-lit eatery. We often stop for pie after finishing our day. Order something unusual and escape the ordinary.

Big Island Dining

Volcano Village

Kiawe Kitchen ✓✓
19-4005 Old Volcano Road
Volcano, HI 96785
808-967-7711
Web: None
Hours: L 12:00 PM-2:30 PM
             D 5:30 PM-9:00 PM
Cards: MC V
Dress: Resort Casual
Style: Continental/Italian $$$

Menu Sampler: Kids Menu Too

Breakfast:
N/A
Lunch/Dinner:
Soup of the Day $6.00, Salad of Mixed Greens with balsamic vinaigrette $6.00, 10" Pizzas: Pizza Margherita, fresh basil, mozzarella and romano $13.00, Pesto Pizza, fresh pesto, mozzarella and romano $14.50, White Pizza, olive oil, garlic, mozzarella and pecorino romano $13.00, Pizza Romana, Margherita with added anchovies and oregano $12.50, additional ingredients $1.50 each
Sandwiches: Gourmet selection available on a 7 inch demi baguette $10.00
Dinner:
Entrees: Fire Roasted Opakapaka with butter & capers served over garlic & scallion smashed potatoes with a ginger beurre blanc and grilled asparagus $26.00, Rack of Lamb (half) served with roasted asparagus and potatoes $26.00, Rib Eye Steak grilled served with roasted garlic and rosemary potatoes $28.00, Linguine and Clams in white wine with garlic, chilli & parsley $20.00, Grilled Pork Loin drizzled with a honey mustard sauce served with fire roasted apples, sweet potatoes and grilled asparagus $21.00, Shrimp Fra Diavolo $22.00
Special Pizzas: Offered daily at both lunch and dinner $18.00 to $19.00
Adult Beverages: Beer/Wine Cellar/Cocktails – Corkage Fee $10.00

Impressions: Intimate Evenings

There's a new dining choice for those who prefer the cool and misty climes of Volcano Village. Owner Mark Kissner recently took responsibility for the old Surt's location next to the local General Store. This dedicated food enthusiast has constructed an Italian-centric menu around items he might serve guests in his home. Not everyone has room for a wood-fired pizza oven in their kitchen, so Mark has installed one for us. We enjoy the cloud country setting. Lunch is good, but evenings are special. Note that they have a $5.00 shared item charge.

Big Island Dining

Volcano Village

Kilauea Lodge & Restaurant ✓✓✓
19-3948 Old Volcano Road
Volcano, HI 96785
808-967-7366
www.kilauealodge.com
Hours: D 5:00 PM-8:45 PM
Cards: MC V
Dress: Resort Casual
Style: Continental/Hawaii Regional $$

Menu Sampler: Kids Menu Too

Breakfast:
Offered for overnight guests only. Not open to the public.
Lunch:
N/A
Dinner:
Starters: Brie Cheese coated in an herb batter with coconut flakes and lightly fried with three grain mini-loaf and brandied apples $8.50, Stuffed Mushroom Caps with seasonings, crab meat, Swiss and cheddar cheeses $8.00, Hand Battered Big Island Zucchini Spears $6.50, Sautéed Mushrooms $8.00
Entrées: served with soup, salad, vegetables and the house three-grain bread, Fresh Catch of the Day prepared three ways; sautéed in piccata sauce, broiled and topped with a papaya ginger sauce or a mango chutney glaze with crushed macadamia nuts or blackened Cajun style with Hawaiian salsa Market Price, Hasenpfeffer, braised rabbit in a hearty hunter's wine sauce $27.50, Lamb Provencal, rack of lamb baked with fresh herbs & seasoned bread crumbs, garnished with papaya apple mint sauce $34.00, Free Range Medallions of Venison flamed with brandy $32.00, Duck L'Orange with apricot mustard glaze $29.00, Osso Buco $37.00, Eggplant Supreme on pasta or rice pilaf $19.50
Adult Beverages: Beer/Wine Cellar/Cocktails

Impressions: Upcountry Oasis

The Kilauea Lodge is located in a former YMCA camp that was refurbished as an inn back in 1987. On a cool, misty upcountry evening you just might get the feeling that you are in British Columbia instead of Hawaii. Out here among the majestic pines and giant ferns the owner/chef prepares an excellent Continental menu backed with touches of Hawaii Regional Cuisine. Patrons can expect rich tastes and large portions from this Old World establishment. Always remember to not over-order. Many guests choose to split an entrée with their partner. You can arrange this for an additional $7.50. Akamai diners always get reservations!

Kohala

Kirin √√
Hilton Waikoloa Village
425 Waikoloa Beach Drive
Waikoloa, HI 96738
808-886-1288
www.hiltonwaikoloavillage.com
Hours: LD 11:00 AM-11:00 PM
Cards: AE DC DIS JCB MC V
Dress: Resort Casual
Style: Dim Sum & Chinese $$

Menu Sampler: Kids Menu Too

Breakfast:
N/A
Lunch/Dinner:
Dim Sum service is provided during lunch with choices from 4.25 to 5.00.
Appetizers: Shrimp and Scallop Rolls (4 pcs) 12.00, Drunken Clams 14.95, Chicken Salad ala Canton 9.50, Jelly Fish 14.50, Five-Spiced Beef 9.50
Soups: Hot and Sour Soup 5.50, "Eight Treasures" Tofu Soup 5.50
Entrées: Prawns with Honey Glazed Walnuts 22.00, Pekingese Scallops 22.00, Szechuan Shrimp 22.00, Szechuan Eggplant with Seafood 18.00, Sizzling Chicken & Shrimp18.00, General Tso's Chicken 14.50, Lemon Chicken 14.50, Peking Duck (half) 25.00, (whole) 48.00, Mu Shu Pork 14.50, Beef Tenderloin ala Cantonese 18.00, Sizzling Scallion Beef 18.00, Mongolian Beef 14.50
Live Seafood: Dungeness Crab sauté with ginger & green onion 22.00/pound, Maine Lobster Baked with Supreme Broth 32.00/pound, Hawaiian Shrimps (white shrimp, shell on) Sautéed with Minced Garlic 28.00/pound, Shrimps Baked with Peppery Salt 28.00/pound, Island Fish, Catch of the Day $Mkt
Vegetables & Tofu: Tofu with Crabmeat 18.00, Choi Sum w/Oyster Sauce 9.50
Noodle & Rice: Yang Chow Fried Rice 10.50, Fried Rice with egg white & Dried Scallop 15.50, Stir Fried Peking Noodle House Style 14.50
Adult Beverages: Beer/Wine Cellar/Cocktails – Corkage Fee 33.00

Impressions: Fine Chinese

Large resort dining rooms have a bad habit of mimicking reality. Not so at Kirin. This upscale Chinese dining venue is a sister restaurant to an old favorite of ours in Honolulu. Things start out with prepared-to-order Dim Sum and progress into the cuisines of Hunan, Szechuan, Peking and Canton. In keeping with traditional standards live seafood is offered. Expect to hear Chinese spoken by the staff and around neighboring tables. Romantics will enjoy the balcony tables by the canal.

Kona

Kona Inn Restaurant ✓✓
Kona Inn Shopping Village
75-5744 Alii Drive
Kailua-Kona, HI 96740
808-329-4455
Web: None
Hours: L 11:30 AM-9:00 PM
        D 5:30 PM-9:00 PM
Cards: AE MC V
Dress: Resort Casual
Style: Steak, Fish & Seafood $$

Menu Sampler: Kids Menu Too

Breakfast:
N/A
Lunch:
Café Grill: 11:30 AM-9:30 PM - Pupus, Soups & Salads and Sandwiches
Soups & Salads: Clam Chowder $4.95/$5.95, Grilled Chicken Caesar Salad
$10.95, Caesar Seafood Salad $6.95, Seafood Cobb Salad $14.95, Poki $7.95
Entrées: Deluxe Burger with chips $8.45, Fresh Fish Sandwich with chips
$Market Price, Sautéed Calamari Sandwich $9.95
Dinner:
Pupus: Sashimi $Mkt Price, Jumbo Shrimp Cocktail w/special sauce $11.95,
Seared Rice Paper Ahi with wasabi dipping sauce $Market Price, Thai Curry
Lemongrass Soup $4.95/$5.95, Field Salad w/Hamakua Goat Cheese $8.95
Entrées: Seafood Pasta on fettucine with vegetables topped with pesto sauce
$20.95, each of the following includes potato, pilaf or rice, green vegetable and
warm bread, Calamari sautéed golden brown $16.95, Hawaiian Chicken, broiled
and topped w/pineapple $17.95, Prime Rib $28.95 & $32.95, Local Fresh Fish
prepared to best present the variety $Market Price, Chef's Specials offered daily
Adult Beverages: Beer/Wine Cellar/Cocktails

Impressions: Romantic Oceanfront

The Kona Inn was built to accommodate inter-island steamship passengers back
during the 1920's. Although the original twenty-room inn is now hidden behind
a garish cluster of shops, the dining room remains in operation. It's actually easy
to find out on a breezy oceanfront point surrounded by a large lawn. A venerable
steak-and-seafood menu has been updated with innovative twists to match tastes
expected today with a setting right out of yesteryear. This romantic dining venue
is a favorite with repeat visitors. Go early and enjoy the magical sunset viewing.

Kona

Kona Pub & Brewery ✓
North Kona Shopping Center
75-5629 Kuakini Highway
Kailua-Kona, HI 96740
808-329-2739
www.konabrewingco.com
Hours: LD 11:00 AM-9:00 PM Su-Th
         LD 11:00 AM-10:00 PM Fr-Sa
Cards: DC DIS MC V
Dress: Casual
Style: American/Island $$

Menu Sampler: Kids Menu Too

Breakfast:
N/A
Lunch/Dinner:
Pupus: Nachos layered with gourmet toppings $9.99, Mac Nut Pesto Cheese
Bread, focaccia topped with macadamia nut pesto, roasted garlic and mozzarella
served with a side of marinara $6.99, Roasted Garlic served with toasted spent
grain focaccia and creamy gorgonzola cheese $5.99, Garlic Twists $3.25
Salads: Caesar Salad $5.49/$7.99, Mauna Loa Spinach Salad tossed in balsamic
vinaigrette with toasted macadamia nuts, chevre, organic tomatoes and red
onions $6.99/9.49, add Grilled Chicken or Rock Shrimp to salad $2.99/$3.99
Sandwiches: all served on house-made focaccia rolls with Kettle Chips, Pololu
sliced chicken breast served hot with mozzarella cheese, roasted red pepper
coulis, pepperoni and fresh basil leaves $8.49, Porterhouse Dip of Roast Beef
marinated and cooked in our Pahoehoe Porter, topped with grilled red onions,
melted cheddar and mozzarella cheeses with porter au jus for dipping $9.99,
Pacific Golden Ale Garlic Shrimp Melt with spinach and cheeses $10.99
Pizza: Small 10", Medium 12" and Large 14" from $8.99 to $22.99, traditional
and gourmet ingredients such as Kalamata olives, macadamia nuts, pesto, wild
mushrooms, roasted red peppers, rock shrimp and lilikoi barbecued chicken
Adult Beverages: Beer/Wine – Corkage Fee $10.00 – Call Ahead

Impressions: Pizza & Pupus

If you enjoy brewpubs you need to swing by the Kona Brewing Company. They
not only produce quality-crafted award-winning beer, their kitchen creates great
pizzas and innovative food. Things start early and run late at this busy gathering
place. Even so, things remain civilized. Look toward the back of the commercial
complex uphill from the King Kamehameha Hotel. Parking is a little spotty here.

Big Island Dining

Kona

La Bourgogne ✓✓✓✓
Kuakini Plaza
77-6400 Nalani Street
Kailua-Kona, HI 96740
808-329-6711
Web: None
Hours: D 6:00 PM-10:00 PM Tu-Sa
Cards: AE DC DIS MC V
Dress: Resort Casual
Style: Classic French $$$

Menu Sampler:

Breakfast/Lunch:
N/A
Dinner:
Appetizers: Pate du chef, house-made mixture, olives, cornichons, moutard $9.00, Escargot de Bourgogne, garlic butter $8.00, Brie au Four wrapped in puff pastry with apple slices and croutons $9.00, Greenlip Mussels steamed in apple cider, white wine, herbs $12.00, Foie Gras et Scallops, raspberry-sherry $16.00
Soups & Salads: French Onion Soup baked with cheese $7.00, House-made Lobster Bisque $8.00, Green Salad with local goat cheese, pine nuts, vinaigrette dressing $10.00, Smoked Duck Breast, roasted pear, greens, raspberry $12.00
Seafood and Poultry: all entrees are served with fresh vegetables of the day and potatoes or wild rice pilaf, Fresh Maine Lobster, braised w/shallots, tomato, brandy, cream $32.00, Scallops sautéed in olive oil, tomato, garlic, basil $28.00
Meat: Slow Roasted Rabbit in white wine, aromatic vegetables, French lavender $28.00, Beef Tenderloin with cabernet sauvignon butter or sauce Béarnaise $32.00, Choice Rack of Lamb with garlic, rosemary butter or Dijon mustard sauce $32.00, Rib Chop of Venison with sherry wine and pomegranate glaze $32.00, Slices of Veal in cream, white wine, shallots, mushroom sauce $27.00
Desserts: Mousse au Chocolate $4.50, Chocolate Grand Marnier Soufflé $6.95
Adult Beverages: Beer/Wine/Cocktails

Impressions: Classic Preps

Habitués of the Kona Coast have long appreciated the culinary cultural transport provided by Chef/Owner Ron Gallaher and his French Country Inn. If soul is the measure of a kitchen then this one ranks near the top. Classic preparations arrive at your table in seamless progression while the fruit of the wine cellar flows into your glass. This traditional continental dining experience is available five nights a week, but the dining room is rather small, so make sure to call for reservations.

Big Island Dining

Volcano Village

Lava Rock Café ✓
19-3972 Old Volcano Road
Volcano, HI 96785
808-967-8526
Web: None
Hours: B 7:30 AM-5:00 PM
        L 10:30 AM-5:00 PM
        D 5:00 PM-9:00 PM Tu-Sa
Cards: MC V
Dress: Casual
Style: American/Island $$

Menu Sampler: Kids Menu Too

Breakfast:
Espresso $3.00, Latte $3.50, Mocha $4.00, Cappuccino $3.50, Sweet Bread
French Toast with homemade lilikoi butter, guava butter or ohelo berry syrup
and 2 eggs $7.45, Pancakes (3) with two eggs $6.95, Three Egg Omelets with
rice or potatoes and toast or biscuit $7.95, Loco Moco $6.25/$7.75

Lunch:
Burgers/Entrées: served with choice of salad, french fries or chips $7.45/$8.50,
Chinese Chicken Salad $8.25, Philly Cheese Steak with choice of salad, french
fries or chips $8.45, Chicken, Steak, Veggie or Tempeh Fajitas $9.45

Dinner:
Dinner Plates: served with soup or garden salad, taro roll, mashed potatoes or
rice and potato-mac salad or cole slaw, Teriyaki Beef $10.25, Hamburger Steak
with gravy and onions $9.75, Chicken Katsu $9.25/$10.75, Kalbi Ribs $12.50
Meals: served with soup and salad, Linguine and Meat Balls w/garlic bread
$10.45, Southern Fried Chicken w/french fries $10.75, New York Steak with
steamed vegetables, choice of baked potato, rice or linguine $14.50, Grilled
Mahi Mahi $13.45, Nightly Specials Tu-Fr $9.95, Prime Rib $17.95/$21.95 Sa
Desserts: Lilikoi, Mango or Ohelo Cheesecake $4.75, Haupia, Dobash or
Pumpkin Crunch $3.95, Hot Fudge Sundae $4.50
Adult Beverages: Beer/Wine/Cocktails

Impressions: Family Menu

Visitors will find this pleasant community gathering place by pulling around the
general store in Volcano Village. The Lava Rock Café serves generous portions
of mainland and island comfort food. Their extensive hours work well for those
who have to drive in from other parts of the island. This is a great place to enjoy
a home-style meal or have a great piece of pie. Route 66 is still alive in Hawaii!

Keauhou

Los Habaneros ✓✓
Keauhou Shopping Center
78-6831 Alii Drive
Kailua-Kona, HI 96740
808-324-4688
Web: None
Hours: BLD 9:00 AM-9:00 PM Mo-Sa
Cards: None
Dress: Casual
Style: Mexican $

Menu Sampler: Kids Menu Too

Breakfast:
Huevos Rancheros 4.99, Eggs Mexican Style 4.99, Egg, Cheese and Salsa Burrito 3.99, Egg, Chorizo and Cheese Burrito 4.25, Add Beans or Rice .75
Lunch/Dinner:
Appetizers: Ceviche, Cocktail Shrimp - Mexican Style, Taquitos, all 5.25
Burritos: choice of refried or black beans, Bean and Cheese 3.99, Chicken, Rice, Cheese, Guacamole 6.50, Carne Asada, Steak, Rice, Beans, Pico de Gallo and Avocado slice 7.50, Fish, Rice, Black Beans, Cheese, Sour Cream 7.75, Served Wet-topped with Enchilada Sauce and Cheese-add .75
Soft or Hard Tacos: Chile Verde, Pork, Lettuce, Cheese 2.50, Ground Beef, Lettuce, Cheese, Sour Cream 2.75, Bean, choice of beans, Lettuce, Cheese 1.99
Other Entrées: Carne Asada, Steak Nachos with Sour Cream and Guacamole 7.75, Chicken Tostada topped with Lettuce, Cheese, Sour Cream, Guacamole 4.25, Veggie Quesadilla, Sautéed Onions, Tomatoes, Zucchini, Mushrooms 6.50 all served with a side of Lettuce, Sour Cream and Guacamole 6.50, Shrimp Enchilada with a side of Rice & choice of Beans, topped with Enchilada Sauce & Cheese 6.99, Steak Taco Salad in a crispy flour tortilla 7.99, Chicken Chimichanga deep fried, stuffed flour tortilla w/Sour Cream, Guacamole 6.99
Adult Beverages: Beer/Margaritas

Impressions: Casually Complete

Have you noticed how Mexican restaurants often fall into one of two categories? First, you've got the fast food joints that offer caricatures instead of cuisine, and then second there are places where both the selections and prices quickly turn up market. It can be hard to find a decently prepared Mexican meal at an affordable price. That's where Los Habaneros comes in. This casual cantina is one of those rare places where you can satisfy that fun food craving without spending a lot of money or selling out to the faux franchises – and they offer it three-meals-a-day!

Big Island Dining

Kona

Manago Hotel Restaurant ✓✓
82-6155 Mamalahoa Hwy (Hwy 11)
Captain Cook, HI 96704
808-323-2642
www.managohotel.com
Hours: B 7:00 AM-9:00 AM XMo
   L 11:00 AM-2:00 PM XMo
   D 5:00 PM-7:30 PM XMo
Cards: DC DIS JCB MC V
Dress: Casual
Style: American/Island $$

Menu Sampler:

Breakfast:
Choice of papaya or juice, coffee or tea, breakfast meat choice of link sausage, Portuguese Sausage, Vienna Sausage, Spam, Ham or Bacon, toast or rice and two eggs $5.50, Pancake $4.00, French Toast $4.00, Hot Tea 1.00, Japanese Green Tea $1.50/$2.50, Hot Chocolate $1.25, Coffee $1.25, Juice $1.25/$1.75

Lunch/Dinner:
Entrées: all entrees include three side dishes and steamed rice, New York Steak $14.00, Shrimp Sauté 11.50, Ahi, Butterfish or Opelo 10.50, Ono, Mahi Mahi or Pork Chops 9.25, Teri Chicken or Beef Teriyaki 8.75, Hamburger Steak 8.00
Sandwiches: all sandwiches come with choice of potato salad or chips, Mahi Mahi $6.25, BLT or Cheeseburger 5.50, Hamburger or Tuna 5.00
Adult Beverages: Beer/Wine/Cocktails

Impressions: Old Hawaii

The Manago Hotel is a "must stop" even if it isn't mealtime. Built in 1917 for traveling salesmen and tourists on their way to the volcano, the Manago looks much the same today as it did two generations ago. Those into time travel can step into the parlor and check out the old photos on the walls. Meanwhile, the Manago offers timeless island comfort food in a dining room that hails back to roadside inns from the 40's and 50's. In fact, the pork chops are a local legend. This entire area is a look at Old Hawaii complete with plantation-era buildings perched along the cliff and the meandering highway cut into the mountainside.

Big Island Dining

Kohala

Mauna Kea Beach Hotel ✓✓✓
62-100 Mauna Kea Beach Drive
Kohala Coast, HI 96743
Manta & Hau Tree: 808-882-5810
Monettes & bar M café: 808-443-2853
www.princeresortshawaii.com
Hours: See Listings
Cards: AE DC DIS JCB MC V
Dress: See Listings
Style: See Listings $$-$$$$

Menu Sampler: Kids Menus Too

Manta:
Sunday Brunch: 11:30 AM-2:00 PM, Resort Casual, Pacific Rim, 48.00/24.00,
fabulous array has always been considered the best on The Big Island of Hawaii
Breakfast: 6:30 AM-11:00 AM, Resort Casual, Pacific Rim, Full Buffet 32.00,
Continental Buffet 26.00, Japanese Bento 27.00, ala carte items 6.00 to 26.00
Dinner: 6:00 PM-9:00 PM, Evening Aloha, Pacific Rim, Ahi Tartar 18, Grilled
Asparagus Salad 14, Kabocha Squash Soup 14, Diver Sea Scallop "BLT" 38
Hau Tree:
Lunch: 11:00 AM- 3:30 PM, Casual, Pacific Rim, Small Plates 8.00 to 16.00
Dinner: 6:00 PM-8:30 PM XSa, Resort Casual, Pacific Rim, Large Plates with
two Side Choices 15.00 to 28.00, Small Plates 8.00 to 16.00, Sides 6.00 to 8.00
Clam Bake: 6:00 PM-9:00 PM Sa, Resort Casual, American, 86.00/43.00
Monettes:
Dinner: 6:00 PM-10:00 PM, Evening Aloha, American French, Kona Kampachi
Carpaccio 19, Keahole Lobster Soup 22, Onaga Snapper Sashimi 18, Opakapaka
44, Duck Breast Seared Crisp 48, Prime Filet Mignon 48, Rack of Lamb 52
bar M café:
Dinner: 5:00 PM-10:00 PM, Resort Casual, Bistro, Small Plates 12 to 19, Large
Plates 22 to 32, On the Side 8 to 12, small and large plates both served ala carte
Adult Beverages: Beer/Wine Cellar/Cocktails

Impressions: Luxury Beachfront

In our opinion the Mauna Kea sits at the pinnacle of Hawaiian resort hotels. The
private beach, a magnificent golf course and exclusive grounds create bookends
for the newly renovated rooms and dining facilities. Highly regarded chefs make
mealtimes an experience instead of an obligation. Menus are designed to appeal
to an international clientele. Note that while the price points are what you would
expect at a venue of this caliber children are catered to at very reasonable levels.

Big Island Dining

Kohala

Merriman's Market Café ✓✓
Kings' Shops
250 Waikoloa Beach Drive
Waikoloa, HI 96738
808-886-1700
www.MerrimansHawaii.com
Hours: LD 11:30 AM-9:00 PM
Cards: AE JCB MC V
Dress: Casual
Style: Mediterranean $$$

Menu Sampler: Kids Menu Too

Breakfast:
N/A
Lunch:
Small Plates: Hummus with warm pita 6.95, Bruschetta and Caponata, herb grilled bread with Sicilian vegetable dip 6.95, Portuguese Cataplana, pan roasted clams with Spanish chorizo, garlic and tomatoes 10.95
Side Salads: Fresh Mozzarella & Vine Ripe Tomatoes, aged balsamic vinegar, extra virgin olive oil 9.95, Caesar w/white anchovies & parmesan crostini 7.95
Sandwiches: Grilled Eggplant & Fresh Basil, goat cheese & spicy harissa on focaccia 8.95, Black Angus 8 oz Ground Chuck Burger with tomato 11.95
Entrées: Big Plate Caesar with Parmesan crostini & Spanish white anchovy 12.95, Waimea Green Salad with pomegranate vinaigrette & roasted pepper currant and walnut relish 13.95, add Grilled Fresh Fish to above 5.00
Dinner:
The entire lunch menu is available plus:
Small Plates: Pizza-ettes with alii mushrooms, white sauce and truffle oil 12.95, Bruschetta & Caponata, grilled country bread with Sicilian eggplant dip 6.95
Salads: Panzanella Italian Bread Salad, tomatoes, onions, pancetta, red wine vinaigrette 9.95, Roasted Beet & Ricotta, champagne vinaigrette, arugula 8.95
Entrées: Tagine Roasted Mahi Mahi Moroccan Style, saffron, olives, preserved lemons and toasted almonds 26.95, Porcini Crusted Flat Iron Steak 28.95
Adult Beverages: Beer/Wine Cellar/Cocktails – Corkage Fee 20.00

Impressions: Cosmopolitan Deli

Peter Merriman has hit several buttons with his new Marketplace Café. In-house guests will find upscale Mediterranean flavors and tastes served in a café setting at competitive prices. Then, as a nod to the condo crowd, the house offers ready-to-cook deli meals that only need to be warmed and served. It's all a step above.

Waimea

Merriman's Restaurant ✓✓✓
Opelo Plaza
65-1227 Opelo Road
Waimea, HI 96743
808-885-6822
www.MerrimansHawaii.com
Hours: L 11:30 AM-1:30 PM Mo-Fr
        D 5:30 PM-9:00 PM
Cards: AE MC V
Dress: Resort Casual
Style: Hawaii Regional/Pacific Rim $$$

Menu Sampler: Kids Menu Too

Breakfast: N/A
Lunch:
Kalua Pig & Sweet Onion Quesadilla, kimchee & mango chili dipping sauce $10.95, Soup of the Day $2.25, Caesar Salad w/grilled fresh island fish $12.95, Chinese Short Ribs, black vinegar braised, Waimea tomato, kim chee, hot mustard, Jasmine rice $12.95, Kalua Pork Barbecue Sandwich, focaccia $9.95
Dinner:
Appetizers: Steamed Kama'aina Manila Clams, Portuguese sausage, garden tomato, parsley, grilled herb bread $12.95, Crispy Lamb Spring Rolls $9.95
Salads: Peter's Original Caesar Salad $8.95, Ahi Tartar, lime-ginger aioli $15.95, Spinach & Smoked Bacon Salad, mushrooms, goat chevre $10.95
Entrées: Merriman's Original Wok Charred Ahi $Market Price, Sautéed Sea Scallops, Waimea spinach, sweet pepper tapenade, lemon caper brown butter, vanilla essence $27.95/$32.95, Hamakua Mushroom Linguini, homegrown arugula, Maui onions, Big Island chevre $23.95, Prime Bone-In New York Steak, Szechuan peppercorn rub, herb garden butter $44.95
Adult Beverages: Beer/Wine Cellar/Cocktails – Corkage Fee $20.00

Impressions: Fusion Lite

Peter Merriman's charming restaurant is located in the town of Waimea just 20 minutes from the resorts on the Kohala Coast. This pioneer in Hawaii Regional Cuisine combines fresh island ingredients in a fusion of flavors and techniques representing every ethnic group in the islands. Check out the shots of his local suppliers in the entryway. We especially like the one of the Puna Goat Cheese vendors posed at their establishment. The sign on the front of the building says "Hippies Use Side Door". This takes on special meaning when you realize that they're all hippies! This view of local color is a great look into Peter's kitchen.

Big Island Dining

Hilo

Naung Mai Thai Kitchen ✓✓

86 Kilauea Avenue
Hilo, HI 96720
808-934-7540
Web: None
Hours: LD 11:00 AM-8:30 PM
Cards: MC V
Dress: Casual
Style: Thai $

Menu Sampler: Kids Spice Level

Breakfast:
N/A

Lunch/Dinner:

Appetizers: Thai Spring Rolls $7.95, Thai Summer Rolls $8.95, Chicken, Pork or Beef Satay $7.95, Fried Tofu $7.95, Savory Prawn Salad $11.95

Salads: Chicken Long Rice Salad $9.95, Naung Mai Beef, Chicken or Pork Larb Salad $8.95, Hot & Sour Seafood Salad $11.95, Cucumber Salad $6.95, Green Papaya Salad $6.95, Shrimp Long Rice Salad $11.95

Soups: Tom Yum Seafood Soup $11.95, Thai Coconut Milk Shrimp Soup $11.95, Thai Long Rice Shrimp Soup $9.95, Tom Yum Vegetarian Soup $8.95

Entrées: served with jasmine or brown rice, Souci Ahi with garlic & fresh chili pepper $13.95, Steamed Salmon with lemon $13.95, Pork Green Curry $10.95, Vegetarian Red Curry $9.95, Beef Massaman Curry $10.95, Cashew Chicken $9.95, Beef Broccoli $9.95, Mixed Seafood with sweet basil $11.95, Chicken or Pork Pad Thai $8.95, Fried Rice Pineapple with Chicken and Shrimp $12.95, Garlic Shrimp $11.95, Pasta with Garlic Basil Chicken $9.95, Chicken Rama $9.95, Eggplant Beef with Thai basil $9.95, Naung Mai Shrimp Fried Rice $11.95, Seafood Padprikgang $11.95, Nua nam tok $9.95, Spicy Basil Beef, Pork or Chicken $9.95, Garlic Shrimp $11.95, Chicken Rama $9.95

Adult Beverages: BYOB

Impressions: Steam & Sizzle

People are always telling us, "We like hole-in-the-walls!" and "Take us more off the beaten track!" Well, here it comes as we present fans with the opportunity to kill two birds with one stone. This local Thai favorite is best approached on foot and would never be confused with a chandeliered dining room. Naung Mai Thai Kitchen serves tasty Thai food authentically prepared at affordable prices. Most of the regulars live around Hilo and aren't phased by these simple surroundings. They were raised on Asian cooking and appreciate elevated but familiar flavors.

Big Island Dining

Hilo

Nihon Restaurant & Cultural Center ✓
123 Lihiwai Street
Hilo, HI 96720
808-969-1133
Web: None
Hours: L 11:00 AM-1:30 PM XSu
        D 5:00 PM-8:00 PM XSu
Cards: AE DC DIS JCB MC V
Dress: Resort Casual
Style: Japanese $$

Menu Sampler: Kids Menu Too

Breakfast:
N/A

Lunch:
The Hatamoto is served with rice, kappa maki, potato salad, konomono, miso soup and tossed salad. Add to this any two entrées from Butterfish Misoyaki, Shrimp Tempura, Sashimi, Broiled Chicken Teriyaki, Tonkatsu, Beef Sirloin Teriyaki, Chicken Katsu $14.95, Oriental Style Shrimp Salad with special miso dressing $10.95, Oyako Donburi of slices of chicken simmered with onions, egg and donburi sauce $8.95, Tofu Nabe with chicken or beef in broth $13.95

Dinner:
Combination Dinner is served with sashimi, rice, konomono, miso soup, Japanese green tea and vegetable salad. Add any two entrées from the above lunch list plus Seafood Batayaki $19.95, Sukiyaki of chicken or beef, vegetables and noodles simmered in an authentic sukiyaki sauce $15.95, Nabeyaki Udon of shrimp tempura, crablet and egg served in a bowl of udon noodles and a light sauce and garnishes $12.95, Nihon Nabemono Specialty of vegetables, seafoods and other garnishes in a light and flavorful broth $16.95, Sushi a la carte
Adult Beverages: Beer/Wine Cellar/Cocktails – No Corkage Fee – Call Ahead

Impressions: Hilo Classic

Food enthusiasts will find this establishment on a peninsula jutting out into Hilo Bay. From the beginning Nihon was conceived to be more than just a restaurant. It's also a cultural center with a small gallery featuring historic photographs and displays. Diners will find reasonably priced local style Japanese cuisine offered in traditional service. For those looking to experience Japanese food and culture as found in Hilo, this would be an interesting choice. One comment though, the restaurant is built on stilts above the tsunami crest. If you have trouble climbing stairs there's an elevator located at the back of the building. Parking is plentiful.

Big Island Dining

Kohala

Norio's ✓✓✓
The Fairmont Orchid, Hawaii
One North Kaniku Drive
Kohala Coast, HI 96743
808-885-2000
www.fairmont.com/orchid
Hours: D 6:00 PM-9:30 PM XTuWe
Cards: AE DC DIS JCB MC V
Dress: Resort Casual
Style: Japanese $$$

Menu Sampler: Kids Menu Too

Breakfast/Lunch:
N/A
Dinner:
Sushi: Chu Toro Nigiri 10, Spicy Hamachi Hand Roll 9, Spider Roll w/soft-shell crab, avocado, kaiware, cucumber & yamagobo 17, Baked Scallop Sushi w/sea scallop baked with cream sauce & tobiko - served with unagi sauce 8, Sashimi Combination chef's choice of assorted sashimi Single 21/ For Two 37
Hot & Cold Appetizers: Tuna Tataki of seared tuna, daikon, Maui onion, wakame seaweed and ponzu sauce with aioli 20, Assorted Tempura 19
Salads: Kaiso assorted seaweed w/sesame vinaigrette 10, Tofu sliced tofu in ponzu sauce 10, Calamari fried calamari w/greens in spicy garlic dressing 16
Entrées: served with rice and miso soup, Lobster and Shrimp Tempura served w/assorted vegetable tempura and ten tsuyu sauce 40, Teriyaki Beef grilled rib-eye w/soba salad and stir-fried vegetables 42, Misoyaki Butterfish w/soba salad and stir-fried vegetables 38, Kushi Katsu of Panko fried pork tenderloin 36
Desserts: Tropical Fruit Fondue of Hawaiian Vintage Chocolate Fondue, apple bananas, golden pineapple and Waimea strawberries 14, Caramel Flan with Asian pear poached in ginger port syrup 10, Green Tea Cheesecake 12
Adult Beverages: Beer/Wine Cellar/Cocktails – Corkage Fee 35 – Call Ahead

Impressions: Happening Place

We're really big on this recent addition to the Kohala dining scene. Like many Hawaii resorts, the Orchid had a large dining area that they devoted primarily to serving their daily breakfast buffet, but left it under-utilized at most other times. Management saw this opportunity and brought in a Japanese dining pro. Norio's vision included adding a full line sushi bar coupled with traditional table service. The end result is a fun, happening place that attracts a cosmopolitan crowd. The sushi chefs are particularly adept at engaging and entertaining a lively audience.

Hilo

Nori's Saimin & Snacks ✓
Kukuau Plaza
688 Kinoole Street
Hilo, HI 96720
808-935-9133
Web: None
Hours: LD 10:30 AM-11:00 PM Tu-Th
          LD 10:30 AM-12:00 AM Fr-Sa
          LD 10:30 AM-10:00 PM Su
Cards: MC V
Dress: Casual
Style: Local/Japanese $

Menu Sampler: Kids Meal Too

Breakfast:
N/A
Lunch/Dinner:
Soups: garnished with green onions, char siu and eggs, Specials include cooked vegetables and a chicken stick on the side, Saimin S $3.75, L $4.45, Udon Won Ton S $4.65, L $5.85, Special $7.10, Seaweed Won Ton Min S $4.65, L $5.85, Mundoo Min S $5.60, L $6.60, Wakana Soba $4.35/$5.05
Noodles: Fried Noodles, Fried Saimin or Chow Fun served with a chicken stick $6.50, Cold Zaru Buckwheat Noodles $6.50, Bi Bim Kook Soo $6.75, Cold Zaru Wakana $6.50, Zaru Udon $6.95
Entrées: include choice of macaroni salad or tossed salad, Teri Beef $7.25, Miso or Korean Butterfish $8.25, Korean Shortribs $7.95, Teri Shrimp or Beef w/Calamari Combo $7.95, Ahi w/choice of four preparations $7.95, Big Plate includes Ahi Tempura, Fried Noodles, Sizzling Salmon Tsukemono Steak w/one scoop of rice, mac salad & a tossed salad $8.25, Pork Cutlet $7.45
Omiyage & Desserts: Nori's Chocolate Mochi by the slice $1.20, mini-loaf $3.95, large loaf $8.95, Nori's Chocolate Mochi Cookies $5.00, Nori's Haupia Pie $1.75, Nori's Mustard Cabbage Koko $3.95, Nori's Mac Nut Brittle $2.95
Adult Beverages: Beer/Wine

Impressions: Local Favorite

Nori's is definitely a cultural experience. It's not the easiest location to pinpoint so you won't find many visitors inside. What you will discover is a very popular local hide-a-way serving a mélange of Hilo-style Japanese and Korean dishes. It might be warm and friendly, but what local people really like are the island kine specialties made as only Nori's can make them. The chocolate mochi cake rules!

Big Island Dining

Hilo

Ocean Sushi ✓✓
250 Keawe Street
Hilo, HI 96720
808-961-6625
Web: None
Hours: L 10:30 AM-2:00 PM XSu
           D 5:00 PM-9:00 PM XSu
Cards: MC V
Dress: Casual
Style: Japanese $

Menu Sampler:

Breakfast:
N/A
Lunch/Dinner:
Nigiri Sushi (2 pcs) Wakame (seaweed salad) $2.50, Ebi (shrimp) $3.00, Unagi (eel) $4.00, Negi Hama (hamachi and green onions) $4.50, Spicy Maguro $3.00
Hosomaki & Temaki: Kappa (cucumber) $1.75, Salmon Skin $3.00, Ahi Poke $3.50, Tako Poke $3.00, California or Canadian $3.00, Unagi Avocado $3.75
Special Rolls: Big Island, ahi, avocado, macadamia nuts, spicy or special mayo $5.00, Mermaid Roll, special scallops (cooked with mayo and flying fish eggs), imitation crab, daikon, shrimp, tobiko on the outside $5.00, Yokohama, in tofu skin, shrimp tempura, imitation crab, avocado, asparagus with mayo or sweet sauce $6.00, Greenbay, smoked salmon, cream cheese and asparagus $5.00, Hamanako, unagi, and cream cheese with kaiware and sesame seeds $6.00
Teishoku: served with rice, miso soup and tsukemono, Shrimp Tempura $9.95, Chicken Teriyaki $7.95, Tonkatsu $8.95, Ahi $9.95, Combo of 2 Items $9.95
Donburi & Curry: Chicken Katsu $7.95, Tonkatsu $8.95, Unagi Don $8.95
Other Favorites: Tempura Udon $7.95, Zaru Soba $5.95, Oxtail Soup $7.95
Side Orders: Gyoza $3.50, Shumai $3.50, Miso Soup $1.00, Edamame $2.50
Sushi Boxes and Family Platters: Extensive selections from $4.75 to $49.95
Adult Beverages: N/A

Impressions: Bustling Hangout

A waitress in a fancy Kohala resort turned us on to this place. She was originally from Hilo and raved about indulging in plates of quality sushi at very reasonable prices. Intrigued by the thought, we did a little research and tracked down Ocean Sushi. The owner of this and a nearby restaurant recently consolidated things by moving the sushi operation into their original space across the street and pooling resources. Japanese dining tradition is followed although with a bit of local spin.

Big Island Dining

Kohala

Pahu i'a ✓✓✓✓
Four Seasons Hualalai Resort
100 Ka'upulehu Drive
Kailua-Kona, HI 96740
808-325-8000
www.fourseasons.com/hualalai
Hours: B 6:30 AM-11:30 AM
          D 6:00 PM-9:30 PM
Cards: AE DC DIS JCB MC V
Dress: Evening Aloha
Style: Pacific Rim $$$$

Menu Sampler: Kids Menu Too

Breakfast:
Big Island Buffet of traditional and alternative breakfast items from 7:00 AM-10:30 AM 32, A la Carte Specials: Huevos Rancheros with Chorizo, refried black beans, corn tortilla, salsa rojo 18, Lemon Ricotta Pancakes 16, Japanese Breakfast 29, Crispy Belgian Waffle with Kahlua Macadamia Nut Butter 16
Lunch: N/A
Dinner:
Appetizers: Pahu i'a Seafood Sampler 24, Kona Cold Lobster Summer Roll 25 Trio of Ahi 23, Kalua Pork Steamed Buns 19, Coconut Crusted Shrimp 20, Big Island Goat Cheese Panna Cotta 22, Hamakua Mushroom Trilogy 18
Entrées: Steamed Opakapaka (Crimson Snapper) ginger, mushrooms, sizzling sesame oil 43, Spicy Crusted Ahi (Yellowfin) soy beans, wasabi salad, balsamic glazed shallots 42, Trio of Hawaiian Jumbo Prawns sweet chili, spicy satay, mac nuts, Tom Yum soup 42, Jumbo Diver Scallops Three Ways daikon-carrot spicy miso, jicama-coconut coconut-orange, ocean salad yellow carrot Kalbi 40, Fire-Roasted 6oz Kobe Beef Tenderloin haricots, mushrooms, tomatoes, chick peas, red wine sauce 120, Prime Dry Aged New York Steak w/potatoes, asparagus & choice of sauce 49, Kurobuta Pork Duet 44, Vegetarian Quartet steamed baby bok choy, grilled mushrooms, sweet corn edamame ragout, chick pea fries 34
Adult Beverages: Beer/Wine Cellar/Cocktails – Corkage Fee 50

Impressions: Truly Oceanfront

Pahu i'a is the eminently luxurious beach house restaurant at the Four Seasons Hualalai Resort. The focus is on fusion cuisine where methods and ingredients from around the world appear in special combinations. Complexity creates the environment for new flavors proving what's inevitable when cultures combine. If there's a romantic in your party, this is a great place for that special evening.

Big Island Dining

Keauhou

Peaberry & Galette √√
Keauhou Shopping Center
78-6831 Alii Drive
Kailua-Kona, HI 96740
808-322-6020
www.peaberryandgalette.com
Hours: 7:000 AM-7:00 PM Mo-Th
7:000 AM-8:00 PM Fr-Sa
8:00 AM-6:00 PM Su
Cards: JCB MC V
Dress: Casual
Style: French/Island $

Menu Sampler:

Breakfast/Lunch:
Savory Crepes: Smoked Salmon, capers, onion with cream cheese $11.50,
Sausage, asparagus and bell pepper w/tomato sauce $12.50, BLT & Egg $10.75,
Avocado and Bacon with sour cream $9.75, Spinach, Mushroom, Ham $10.75
Dessert Crepes: Crepe Suzette $7.50, Chocolate Banana with vanilla ice cream
$8.50, Caramelized Apple with vanilla ice cream $8.50, Café Mocha, ice cream
$7.50, Fresh Strawberry & jam, custard sauce $8.50, Fruits, yogurt, honey $9.00
Sandwich & Other Meals: BLT Egg Sandwich $7.25, Tofu Salad $5.75, Salad
Nicoise $9.75, Quiche Lorraine $4.50, Calamari & Shiso leaf pasta $13.75,
Breaded Hamburger Sandwich $6.00, Ham or Turkey Sandwich $7.25
Homemade Cakes & Other Sweets: Strawberry Shortcake $4.50, Lemon Bar
$2.75, Chocolate Banana Parfait $4.75, Baked Chocolate Cheesecake $3.75,
Chocolate Banana Parfait $4.75, Strawberry Parfait $4.75, Muffins, Cookies
Coffee, Tea & Other Refreshments: Espresso, Café Latte, Café Mocha,
Americano, Caramel Marcchiato, PB&G private 100% pure Kona coffee,
variety of loose teas, Monin Syrups & Ghirardelli Chocolate
Adult Beverages: N/A

Impressions: Kona Creperie

The Big Island of Hawaii seems to attract and support alternative dining venues
that don't work on the other islands. This is a great example. Someone took the
Creperie concept found on every street corner in France, transported it to a sun
baked ridge in Keauhou, added Kona Coffee, and it takes off! Perhaps the chef
understands that sweet and savory crepes should have different batters, or plain
luck is involved, but it's nice to see an original idea thrive in our homogenized
world. The crepes are made to order so check out the art gallery while you wait.

Big Island Dining

Hilo

Pescatore ✓✓
235 Keawe Street
Hilo, HI 96720
808-969-9090
Web: None
Hours: B 7:30 AM-11:00 AM Sa-Su
          L 11:00 AM-2:00 PM
          D 5:30 PM-9:00 PM
Cards: AE DC DIS JCB MC V
Dress: Resort Casual
Style: Italian $$$

Menu Sampler: Kids Menu Too

Breakfast:
French Toast 4.95, with fresh strawberries & cream 5.25, Italian Omelet with Italian sausage, Fern Forest spinach, mushrooms, tomatoes and cheddar cheese topped with marinara sauce and served with home fries or rice 6.95

Lunch:
Panini Grill Sandwiches with fries or pasta salad: Grilled Chicken w/ prosciutto, provolone, fresh sage, roasted pepper mayonnaise 8.95, Veggie Panini of grilled portobellos, spinach, garlic, roasted peppers and fresh mozzarella 7.50
Pizza: 8" & 12" 8.95 to 18.95 with traditional and gourmet toppings
Pasta: Pesto 4.25/5.95, Alfredo 5.95/8.95, Puttanesca 4.95/7.95

Dinner:
Antipasti: Carpaccio de Pesce of ahi with garlic, capers, red onion, balsamic vinegar, olive oil & Parmesan 10, Calamari 7, Sautéed Artichokes 6.00
Pasta: Puttanesca (includes soup or salad) olive oil, garlic, anchovies, capers, crushed red peppers, sun dried tomatoes and olives 16, Fra Diavolo 19.00
Entrées: includes soup or salad and fresh baked bread, Veal Scaloppini Marsala 24, Cioppino Classico 28, Lamb Chops marinated with mint pesto 28, Black Angus Ribeye Steak Grilled 27, Chicken Breast Parmesan Style 18, Fisherman's Platter, fish parmigian, shrimp scampi and calamari 22
Adult Beverages: Beer/Wine Cellar/Cocktails – Corkage Fee 10

Impressions: Old Italy

Pescatore is in the old part of downtown Hilo. With its high ceilings, bentwood chairs and the evening mist falling outside one gets the feeling of being in a big city neighborhood instead of Hawaii. Expect a traditional Italian menu with all the regional classics. The black tie service sets an appropriate mood. Prices fall outside the budget category, but you can spend much more for a whole lot less.

Big Island Dining

Kona

Quinn's Almost By The Sea √√

75-5655 Palani Road
Kailua-Kona, HI 96740
808-329-3822
Web: None
Hours: L 11:00 AM-5:00 PM
        D 5:00 PM-10:30 PM
Cards: MC V
Dress: Casual
Style: American/Seafood $$

Menu Sampler: Kids Menu Too

Breakfast:
N/A

Lunch:
Pupus: Sautéed Mushrooms w/garlic bread in brandy and garlic butter 6.95, Quinn's Spicy or Korean Wings 8.95, Crab Stuffed Mushrooms 10.50, Kalbi Pupu 10.95, Broiled Steak Strips, 5 oz. Filet Mignon topped w/grilled onions 11.50, Deep Fry Pork Egg Rolls with sweet chili sauce 9.50
Burgers: served with fries, rice or salad, Char Broiled Burger 8.50
Sandwiches: served with fries, rice or salad, Snow Crab Mix on Sourdough with jack cheese 11.25, Mahi Mahi on an onion bun 10.25, Monte Cristo 9.50
Soups & Salads: Clam Chowder 2.95/3.95, Shrimp & Crab Salad $11.95

Dinner:
All of the above available plus the following served with soup or dinner salad, vegetable and choice of rice, Quinn's Potatoes or fries - Catch of the Day 23.50, Teriyaki Chicken smothered in mushrooms 18.95, Shrimp Scampi on a bed of linguine 22.95, Steak & Broiled Shrimp 23.95, Filet Mignon 22.95
Adult Beverages: Beer/Wine/Cocktails

Impressions: Late Night

Across from the King Kamehameha Hotel you'll find an old Kailua-Kona haunt that looks deceptively small from the street. Upon entering the establishment an attractive courtyard patio and a respectable sized dining room reveal themselves. The décor is "island funky" reminiscent of the Florida Keys. This unpretentious hideaway serves good food at very convenient hours in a hospitable atmosphere. After 9 PM it can be difficult to find restaurants that are still open on this island, but Quinn's serves until late. So whether your body clock is all turned around or you simply stayed too long after happy hour, take a stroll up Alii Drive and give Quinn's a try for a casual late evening dinner. Parking is scarce so use a pay lot.

Big Island Dining

Kona

Rapanui Island Café ✓✓
Kona Banyan Court
75-5695 Alii Drive
Kailua-Kona, HI 96740
808-329-0511
Web: None
Hours: D 5:00 PM-9:00 PM Mo-Sa
Cards: MC V
Dress: Casual
Style: Island $$

Menu Sampler:

Breakfast/Lunch:
N/A

Dinner:

Pupus: Duck Wontons with dipping sauces $6.95, Green Flash Mussels with chilies, shallots, garlic and lime $8.95, Spring Rolls with veggies and rice noodles seasoned with spices, deep fried, served with dipping sauces $4.95

Salads: Gado Gado, layered salad of fresh cucumbers, green beans, carrots, cherry tomatoes, sprouts and tofu with peanut sauce $11.95, with shrimp $15.95, Kakariki, green salad of spinach, cucumbers, green beans, pea sprouts and tofu, dressed with a hoisin lime vinaigrette $9.95

Entrées: all main courses are served with your choice of rice and cucumber salad, Moa Chicken marinated in white wine, garlic, shallots, tarragon and rosemary, grilled, peanut sauce $14.95, Beef Cashew with caramelized onions, garlic, broccoli $12.95, Spiced Pork with green and red chilies, coconut milk $12.95, Macadamia Shrimp Stir Fry with vegetables and peanut sauce $14.95, Fresh Island Catch Stir Fry with vegetables, sesame, garlic, cashews $16.95

Vegetables: Tofu Stir Fry with vegetables and vegetarian garlic soy sauce $11.95, Curry of Vegetables in a red curry sauce with tomato and lime banana $12.95, Julienne Vegetable Stirfry with vegetarian garlic soy sauce $9.95

Combination Plates: Rua-fresh island fish & seafood seared w/garlic, veggies, island salsa, soy glaze $Mkt, Wha, combination sate with peanut sauce $15.95

Adult Beverages: N/A

Impressions: Exotic Tastes

Those who remember when Sibu Café served the best health food plates on Alii Drive will appreciate this place more than most. Not only is it located in the old Sibu space, but the culinary fare is even better than ever. The current proprietor once cooked at Sibu and broadened their menu while maintaining the standards.

Kona

Royal Jade Garden ✓✓
Lanihau Center
75-5595 Palani Road
Kailua-Kona, HI 96740
808-326-7288
Web: None
Hours: LD 10:30 AM-9:00 PM
Cards: JCB MC V
Dress: Casual
Style: Chinese $

Menu Sampler:

Breakfast:
N/A
Lunch/Dinner:
Appetizers: Royal Jade Platter S 10.50, L 16.95, Egg Roll 3.95, Crisp Won Ton 4.95, Pot Stickers 6.95, Char Siu 5.95, Fried Shrimp 6.95, Gau Gee 6.95
Soups: Abalone Soup 10.95, Pork with Watercress Soup 7.95, Hot & Sour Soup $7.50, Chicken Cream Corn Soup 7.50, Ox Tail Soup 8.95, Seaweed Soup 7.95
Entrées: Fried Tofu Vegetable Black Bean Sauce 8.95, Cashew Nut Vegetable 7.95, Beef with Oyster Sauce 7.95, Steamed Pork Hash 8.25, Roast Duck 8.50, Kung Pao Chicken 7.95, Chicken with Cashew Nuts 8.25, Fish Filet with Vegetables 9.25, Pineapple Shrimp 8.95, Abalone w/Mustard Greens 14.95, Honey Glazed Walnut Shrimp 9.95, Royal Jade Chow Mein 8.95, Beef Chow Fun 7.95, Vegetarian Egg Fu Yong 7.95, Grandma's Tofu (spicy) 8.25, Shrimp a la Canton 8.95, Char Siu 8.25, Scallop w/Chinese Peas 8.95, Chicken Curry 7.95
House Specials: Garlic Shrimp Hong Kong Style 10.50, Mandarin Sweet and Sour Chicken 8.95, Mongolian Lamb 9.95, Duck w/Mustard Cabbage 9.95
Noodles: Royal Jade Wor Mein Soup 7.50, Char Siu Sai Mein 4.95, Wor Won Ton Mein 7.25, Spicy Beef Mein 7.50, Gau Gee Mein Soup 6.50
Rice: Char Siu, Beef, or Chicken Fried Rice 6.95, Shrimp Fried Rice 7.50, Royal Jade Fried Rice 7.50, Steamed Rice 1.25, Seafood Fried Rice 8.95
Adult Beverages: Beer/Wine

Impressions: Extensive Menu

Don't be put off by the shopping plaza location - Royal Jade Garden is no Takee Outee. This family-owned establishment offers a wide range of Chinese classics with some unusual items presented for additional interest. They offer a buffet to the hurry-up crowd at lunch, but we always prefer to order from the menu. It all seems to play out better that way. Make sure to inquire about the daily specials.

Big Island Dining

Hilo

Royal Siam Thai ✓
70 Mamo Street
Hilo, HI 96720
808-961-6100
Web: None
Hours: L 11:00 AM-2:00 PM XSu
        D 5:00 PM-8:30 PM
Cards: AE DC DIS MC V
Dress: Casual
Style: Thai $$

Menu Sampler:

Breakfast:
N/A

Lunch/Dinner:
Appetizers: Fried Fresh Tofu with spicy Thai sauces 5.95, Spring Rolls with sweet and sour sauce 6.95, Chicken Satay with peanut sauce 6.95, Royal Siam Crispy Chicken with lemongrass, ginger, garlic and sweet sour sauce 6.95
Soups: Thom Yum Seafood Soup with a tangy broth of spices, straw mushrooms, tomatoes, lemongrass, lime leaves and vegetables in mild, medium or hot 9.95, Coconut Chicken Soup 7.95, Thai Noodle Soup with Chicken 7.95
Salads: mild, medium or hot, Green Papaya Salad 6.50, Cucumber Salad 6.50, Royal Siam Tofu Salad 7.95, Hot & Sour Shrimp or Squid Salad 9.95
Entrées: mild, medium or hot, Budda Rama-chicken sautéed in peanut sauce on a bed of spinach 8.95, Red Curry with chicken or beef and bamboo or eggplant 8.95, Scallops with sweet basil 10.95, Thai Garlic Shrimp 10.95, Ginger Chicken, Beef or Pork 8.95, Yellow Curry with Chicken or Beef with potatoes and onions 8.95, Seafood Curry of shrimp, scallop, calamari & fish with yellow curry, vegetables and rice 10.95, Eggplant with Chicken 8.95, Cashew Chicken 8.95, Basil Chicken or Beef 8.95, Ong Choi Beef 8.95
Rice and Noodles: Thai Broccoli Noodles with chicken, beef, pork 7.95
Desserts & Drinks: Tapioca Pudding 2.50, Thai Iced Tea or Coffee 1.95
Adult Beverages: Beer/Wine

Impressions: Solid Thai

Visitors and locals alike enjoy this small eatery in downtown Hilo. Their service is fast, prices reasonable and they've won awards for the consistently good Thai cuisine. All the favorites are offered with comforting tastes paired alongside an occasional spicy surprise. The menu is lengthy but they are known to offer some dishes that are only prepared upon request. Curbside parking is usually plentiful.

Big Island Dining

Kohala

Roy's Waikoloa Bar & Grill ✓✓✓
King's Shops
250 Waikoloa Beach Drive
Waikoloa, HI 96738
808-886-4321
www.roysrestaurant.com
Hours: D 5:00 PM-9:30 PM
Cards: AE DC JCB MC V
Dress: Resort Casual
Style: Hawaiian Fusion $$$

Menu Sampler: Kids Menu Too

Breakfast/Lunch:
N/A
Dinner:
Appetizers & Salads: Caramelized Leek & Sweet Corn Soup, truffle oil drizzle, saffron crème fraiche 6.50, Char Siu Spring Rolls with long rice noodles, roasted peanut chili sauce 11.00, Asian Style Sesame Crab & Romaine Salad, wasabi garlic dressing, seasoned nori, tobiko caviar 9.50
Yamaguchi Sushi: "Da Paniolo" Roll, filet of beef, crab meat, roasted red bell pepper, Jackie's spicy barbecue sauce 15.00, Fresh Island Fish Roll, Island Ahi Kampachi, Ted Tai Snapper, Li Hing daikon 15.00, Green Flash Vegetable Roll, soy paper, sesame Shiitake mushrooms, mixed greens 8.50, Trio Roll 12.50
Entrées: Roy's Classic Macadamia Nut Crusted Monchong in a Kona Maine Lobster Essence 31.50, Furikake Crusted Shrimp, sesame soy Asian noodle stir fry, sweet soy sauce 29.50, Spicy Pancetta Crusted Ono, roasted eggplant ratatouille, green beans, oyster sesame glaze 32.50, Roy's Waikoloa Roasted Duck, scallion-cilantro pancakes and a smoky hoisin glaze 28.50, Balsamic Grilled 12 oz. Ribeye, Big Island Goat Cheese Mash, Crispy Onion Rings 32.50, Roy's Szechuan Style Baby Back Ribs & Pineapple Chili White Shrimp 31.50
Desserts: Wonderful tray of gourmet desserts changing daily!
Adult Beverages: Beer/Wine Cellar/Cocktails – Corkage Fee 20.00

Impressions: Fusion Favorite

We've never had a bad experience at Roy's—regardless of which location! Roy Yamaguchi was one of the founders of the Hawaii Regional Cuisine movement. Restaurants bearing his name are now found worldwide. Fresh local ingredients combined with taste-pleasing twists make dining at Roy's a culinary experience worth going out of your way. Trademark sauces and presentations appear on all of Roy's menus, but dishes unique to each venue highlight the chef's creativity.

Big Island Dining

Kohala Coast

Ruth's Chris Steak House ✓✓✓
The Shops at Mauna Lani
68-1330 Mauna Lani Drive
Kohala Coast, HI 96743
808-887-0800
www.ruthschris.com
Hours: D 5:00 PM-9:30 PM
Cards: AE DC JCB MC V
Dress: Resort Casual
Style: Steak $$$$

Menu Sampler: Kids Menu Too

Breakfast/Lunch:
N/A
Dinner:
Appetizers: Barbecued Shrimp sautéed in reduced white wine, butter, garlic and spices $13.95, Seared Ahi/Sashimi in a sauce of ginger, mustard, beer $Mkt, Sizzlin' Blue Crab Cakes with lemon butter $19.50, Lobster Bisque $12.50, Onion Soup Au Gratin $9.95, Veal Osso Buco Ravioli, demi glace $13.95
Salads: Spinach Salad with red onion, mushrooms, crisp bacon, chopped egg and warm bacon dressing $5.50/$8.50, Ruth's Chop Salad $6.95/$9.95
Entrées: Filet $39.95, Petite Filet $35.95, Ribeye $42.95, Bone-In Ribeye $45.95, New York Strip $43.95, T-Bone $48.95, Veal Chop with Sweet and Hot Peppers $36.95, Pork Porterhouse $32.95, Petite Filet and Shrimp $48.95, Fresh Lobster 2.5-5 pounds $Mkt, Lamb Chops cut extra thick $40.95, Broiled Marinated Chicken $25.95, Cold Water Lobster Tails $Mkt
Sides: Potatoes, Mashed with roasted garlic, Baked, Lyonnaise, Cottage, Julienne, Shoestring $7.95, Sweet Potato Casserole with a pecan crust $8.95, Potatoes Au Gratin $8.95, Fresh Spinach Creamed or Au Gratin $8.95, Fresh Broccoli $7.95, Fresh Broccoli Au Gratin $8.95, Sautéed Mushrooms $7.95
Adult Beverages: Beer/Wine Cellar/Cocktails

Impressions: Always Reliable

Layering is big in the restaurant industry. Fusion cuisine utilizes ingredients and methods not commonly matched and "layers" them to create exciting new tastes. Vertical preparations take that approach another step by stacking components in "layers" to further enhance the complexity and contrast. Then there's the Ruth's Chris operandi where absolutely decadent courses are offered ala carte allowing the diner to design his own combination of favorite flavors. This total Epicurean experience doesn't come cheap, but don't miss out if it's somebody else's treat!

Big Island Dining

Kohala

Sansei Seafood Restaurant & Sushi Bar ✓✓✓

Queen's Market Place
Waikoloa Beach Resort
201 Waikoloa Beach Drive
Waikoloa, HI 96738
808-886-6286
www.sanseihawaii.com
Hours: D 5:30 PM-10:00 PM
         Late D 10:00 PM-1:00 AM FrSa
Cards: AE DIS MC V
Dress: Resort Casual
Style: Pacific Rim/Seafood $$$

Menu Sampler: Kids Menu Too

Breakfast/Lunch:
N/A
Dinner:
Sushi & Sashimi: Mango and Crab Salad Hand Roll $9.95, Panko Crusted Ahi Sashimi Sushi Roll $11.95, Yellow Submarine Roll $7.95, Rainbow Roll $12.95, Spicy Hamachi Roll $6.50, Flower Sushi, Nigiri Sushi & Sashimi Market Price
Starters: Crispy Fried Calamari $8.95, Sansei's Lobster & Blue Crab Ravioli $10.95, Sansho-Crusted Ahi Tataki $14.00, Japanese Hamachi Nori Aioli Poke $13.00, Sansei's Asian Shrimp Cake $7.95, Wok Tossed Big Island Vegetables $7.95, Grilled Hamakua Shiitake Mushrooms $7.95, Shrimp Dynamite $11.95
Soup & Salad: Sansei's Ramen Noodles $9.95, Hiyashi Seaweed Salad $4.95, Japanese Calamari Salad $10.95, Seared Ahi Salad $11.95, Miso Soup $2.95
Entrées: Chef Omakase Tasting Menu for Two $70.00, Ginger Hoisin Smoked Duck Breast $24.95, Roasted Japanese Jerk-spiced Chicken $21.95, Shichimi Crusted Beef Filet & Udon Noodles $28.95, Big Island Vegetable Pasta $15.95
Desserts: "Granny Smith" Apple Tart $8.95, Tempura Fried Macadamia Nut Ice Cream $8.95, Crème Brulee $6.95, Hawaii Ice Cream or Fruit Sorbet $5.95
Adult Beverages: Beer/Wine Cellar/Cocktails

Impressions: Nouveau Sushi

Chef/Owner D.K. Kodama has won numerous awards for his unique approach to Pacific Rim cuisine. Here at Sansei's new Waikoloa Resort restaurant diners can experience his intriguing creations and their contemporary Japanese vitality. The innovative yet reasonably priced sushi and entrées have made this a great choice for locals and visitors alike. Dining at Sansei is grazing at its best. In addition to the usual bar service they have a fine selection of sake. Come late for a discount.

Big Island Dining

Hilo

Seaside Restaurant ✓✓
1790 Kalanianaole Avenue
Hilo, HI 96720
808-935-8825
www.seasiderestaurant.com

Hours:	D 5:00 PM-8:30 PM Su Tu-Th
	D 5:00 PM-9:00 PM Fr-Sa
Cards:	AE DC JCB MC V
Dress:	Resort Casual
Style:	Island $$

Menu Sampler: Kids Menu Too

Breakfast/Lunch:
N/A

Dinner:

Pupus: Sautéed Mushrooms in butter and garlic $7.50, Calamari Strips $8.95, Shrimp Cocktail, seven shrimp w/sauce $8.95, Steamed Manila Clams $11.50

Sushi: Spider Roll $9.75, Volcano Shrimp Roll $7.50, Spicy Tuna Roll $6.95, Tekka Maki $3.50, Unagi Roll $9.00, California Roll $5.00, Ahi Poke $8.50

Complete Dinners: include fresh salad, sautéed vegetables, rice or pasta with butter and garlic sauce, Steamed Mullet $21.95/$26.95, Fried Aholehole with daikon-suri $24.95, Furikake Salmon served with teriyaki sauce and wasabi mayonnaise aioli $21.95, Shrimp Scampi sautéed in a butter garlic sauce served with linguini and sautéed vegetables $19.95, Grilled Lamb Chops served with a poha mint sauce $30.95, New York Steak and Lobster served w/drawn butter & lemon $Mkt, Kiawe Grilled New York Steak w/onions & mushrooms $21.95

Specials: Volcano Shrimp-filo wrapped with mango mint chili sauce $22.95, Chinese Style Steamed Kona Kampachi $27.95, Pan Fried Moi $27.95

Desserts: Taro and Sweet Potato Bread Pudding $5.95, Cherries Jubilee $5.95, Kona Coffee Mud Pie $5.95, Hilo Homemade Gourmet Ice Cream $3.75

Adult Beverages: Beer/Wine Cellar/Cocktails – Corkage Fee $20.00

Impressions: Aquatic Adventure

Along the coastline just south of the airport you'll find a Hilo institution. The Seaside Restaurant is unique among Hawaii's seafood eateries as it sits on the edge of an ancient fishpond that still operates as an aquaculture farm for their kitchen. Naturally, "When in Rome" is the order of the day here, so figure on trying one of their fresh fish dishes. Besides a wide array of mainstream items the menu presents creative options you seldom find offered. Add considerable depth of preparation to what could be a simple table and it's hard to go wrong.

Big Island Dining

Waimea

Solimene's ✓✓

Waimea Shopping Center
65-1158 Mamalahoa Hwy (Hwy 19)
Waimea, HI 96743
808-887-1313
Web: None
Hours: L 11:00 AM-3:00 PM
        D 5:00 PM-9:00 PM
Cards: AE DC DIS JCB MC V
Dress: Casual
Style: Italian $$

Menu Sampler:

Breakfast:
N/A
Lunch:
Hot Meatball Parmigiana or Hot Pastrami Sandwich with choice of pasta salad or garden salad $8.95, Soup of the Day $2.95/$4.95, Caesar Salad $10.95
Dinner:
Antipasti: Creamy Baked Goat Cheese Topped with Figs and Caramelized Onions w/Crostini $9.95, Jumbo Crispy Crab Ravioli w/mango chili sauce $9.95
Insalate: Garden $6.95, Solimene's House of fresh Kamuela greens, sliced pears, candied walnuts, gorgonzola, raspberry vinaigrette $10.95
Pizza: in personal, medium, large $6.95 to $26.95 with a variety of toppings
Entrées: Chicken Parmigiana with a side of spaghetti and vegetable of the day $13.95, Shrimp Scampi over linguine with garlic bread $16.95, Salmon cooked with lemon, butter, capers and fresh herbs over pasta or garlic mashed potatoes, vegetable $17.95, New York Steak, spaghetti or potatoes, vegetable $21.95, Crab Agnolotti in butter wine sauce with scallops & arugula, garlic bread $19.95
Desserts: Caramel Turtle Cheesecake $4.25, Warm Molten Chocolate Dome Cake $5.95, Tiramisu $6.95, Chocolate Hazelnut Calzone $7.95
Adult Beverages: Beer/Wine

Impressions: Grandma's Recipes

Waimea is one of those unique small communities that can attract and support a wide variety of culinary establishments. Why? Dust off the cowboy exterior and you'll find major league bank balances! Solimene's was a recent addition to this neighborhood mix bringing a higher level of Italian cuisine to a simple shopping center storefront. The informal nature of the place creates a mama's kitchen feel, but the complexity of the menu reassures you that it's more than a panini palace.

Hilo

Sombat's ✓✓✓
88 Kanoelehua Ave
Hilo, HI 96720
808-969-9336
www.sombats.com

Hours: L 10:30 AM-2:00 PM Mo-Fr
            D 5:00 PM-9:00 PM Mo-Sa
Cards: AE DC DIS JCB MC V
Dress: Casual
Style: Thai $$

Menu Sampler:

Breakfast:
N/A
Lunch/Dinner:
Lunch Hot Bar - One Choice $6.00, Two Choices $7.00, Three Choices $8.00
Appetizers: Deep Fried Spring Rolls $7.95, Fresh Basil Rolls with shrimp or tofu $7.95, Chicken Satay with peanut sauce $7.95, Fried Tofu $7.95
Salads: Somtum $7.95, Chicken Salad $9.95, Shrimp or Squid Salad $11.95
Soups: Chicken Tom Yum $9.95, Seafood Combo Coco Soup w/onions $15.95
Noodles: Chicken Pad Thai $9.95, Shrimp Pad Lard Nah with broccoli $11.95
Rice: Beef Spicy Fried Rice with green chili, onion, mint or basil leaves $9.95
Curries: Chicken Kang Panang roasted curry with coconut milk and string beans $10.95, Shrimp Kang Ped red curry w/bamboo shoots, sweet basil $13.95
Meat & Vegetable Stir Fry: Pork Garlic and Pepper with ground garlic, black pepper and sweet black sauce $10.95, Seafood Combo in roasted curry paste, cashew nut dressing $10.95, Beef w/Eggplant, fresh basil, soybean sauce $10.95
Vegetarian Specialties: Large selection of soups and main dishes all at $10.95
Ala Carte: Steamed Jasmine or Brown Rice $2.00, Steamed Sticky Rice $2.50
Adult Beverages: N/A – No Corkage Fee

Impressions: Curry Bomb

Those staying at the Banyan Drive hotels have an unexpected pleasure waiting for them within walking distance. Facing the highway in the commercial plaza next to Ken's House of Pancakes you'll find a small Thai place with big tastes. This is Sombat's realm where everything but the complexity that creates flavor has been scaled down to Hilo dimensions. Instead, additional touches appear in the dishes taking the experience to a higher level. Resist the temptation to over-order. One main entrée with rice feeds two nicely, and the soup is family-sized. Dishes are offered mild, medium, hot and Thai hot. Watch out for that last one!

Big Island Dining

Kona

Sushi Shiono ✓✓✓
Sunset Alii Plaza
75-5799 Alii Drive
Kailua-Kona, HI 96740
808-326-1696
Web: None
Hours: L 11:30 AM-2:00 PM Mo-Fr
          D 5:30 PM-9:00 PM Mo-Sa
Cards: AE DC DIS JCB MC V
Dress: Casual
Style: Japanese $$$

Menu Sampler:

Breakfast:
N/A
Lunch:
Teriyaki Chicken and Tempura or Ahi Katsu with miso soup, salad and rice 9.5, Ton Katsu with miso soup, salad and rice 9, Fried Mackerel Japanese Style with miso soup and salad 8.5, Shiono Sushi Special with miso soup and salad 15
Dinner:
Sushi: Maguro 7, Toro 15, Unagi 6, Ika 6, Ama Ebi 9, Hotate 7, Tamago 5, Shrimp Tempura Roll 9, Rainbow Roll 15, Spicy Hawaiian Volcano Roll 15
Starters: Edamame 3.5, Seafood Salad with mixed greens and tobiko 12, Dynamite baked with aioli sauce 15, Poke with seaweed and soy dressing 15
Noodles: Hot Shrimp & Veg. Tempura Udon or Soba with 3 pc. California Roll 10, Cold Udon or Soba Noodles with dipping sauce and 3 pc. California Roll 7.5
Entrées: all entrées served with miso soup, salad and rice, 10 oz Grilled NY strip steak and vegetable with ponzu or teri sauce 25, Broiled Mackerel or Salmon 20, Ton-Katsu of panko breaded pork cutlet 20, Beef & Reef Combo of a 5 oz steak with sautéed mixed vegetables and choice of California or spicy tuna roll and 4 pieces of Nigiri 30, Unagi Kabayaki-grilled freshwater eel 22
Sweets: Tempura Ice Cream with pound cake, chocolate and raspberry sauce 7
Adult Beverages: Beer/Sake/Wine – Corkage Fee 25

Impressions: Upscale Ambiance

Time works in funny ways. Some things improve over time while others decline. There's been a sushi parlor in this location for as long as we can remember, but we've never known it to shine like it does today. New is the operative word, and expect it everywhere from the menu to the furnishings. Naturally Japanese chefs make the room work by preparing authentic dishes appropriate for all audiences.

Big Island Dining

Waimea

Tako Taco ✓✓
64-1066 Mamalahoa Hwy (Hwy 19)
Waimea, HI 96743
808-887-1717
www.takotaco.com
Hours: LD 11:00 AM-8:30 PM Mo-Sa
       LD 12:00 PM-8:00 PM Su
Cards: AE MC V
Dress: Casual
Style: Mexican $

Menu Sampler: Kids Menu Too

Breakfast:
N/A
Lunch/Dinner:
Salads: Fish Salad, local greens, grilled fish, local tomatoes, red onion, cucumber, carrots, Pico de Gallo salsa, guacamole $8.75, Taco Salad $8.25
Entrées: Taco with choice of meat, grilled marinated chicken, ground beef, carnitas (slow roasted cubes of pork) Taco meat or chile verde, choice of black or pinto beans, toppings $3.50, Fish Taco Plate, 2 grilled fish tacos, Mexican rice, choice of black or pinto beans $8.75, Cheese Quesadilla $3.95, Quesadilla, Two flour tortillas, Monterey Jack cheese, caramelized onion, sautéed mushrooms, guacamole, sour cream $6.95, Astro-Nachos, topped with choice of black or pinto beans, melted Monterey jack cheese, guacamole, sour cream, Pico de Gallo salsa $5.25/$8.95, Super Paniolo Burrito, meat, beans, rice, cheese, guacamole, sour cream, salsa $8.75, Tostadas, meat, beans, cheese, shredded cabbage, salsa $4.75, Vegetarian Burrito, beans, rice, salsa $4.50,Tofu Burrito, tofu in ranchero sauce, beans, rice, shredded cabbage, and salsa $6.50
House Specialties: Chicken Enchilada Plate topped with green chili sauce $11.50, Cheese Enchilada Plate $8.95, Grilled Steak Taco Plate $10.25
Adult Beverages: Beer/Wine/Margaritas

Impressions: Family Value

Long-time travelers may have noticed something we refer to as "Seb'n Dollah" This is the minimum price an island businessman can charge and still cover his overhead. We first identified this phenomenon in Nassau where no matter how far you had to go the cab fare was always "Seb'n Dollah". The same applies in Hawaii where high rents usually dictate a high minimum price-per-customer. If you have a herd of hungry kids and want to avoid feeding the landlord consider Tako Taco where family fare at budget price is the special-of-the-day everyday.

Big Island Dining

Kona

Teshima Restaurant ✓✓
79-7251 Mamalahoa Hwy (Hwy 11)
Honalo, HI 96750
808-322-9140
Web: None
Hours: B 6:30 AM-11:00 AM
        L 11:00 AM-1:45 PM
        D 5:00 PM-9:00PM
Cards: None
Dress: Casual
Style: American/Japanese $

Menu Sampler:

Breakfast:
Two Eggs, Meat, choice of two: toast, hash browns or rice $4.75, Fried Rice w/ two eggs and ham $7.75, Japanese Breakfast of fried fish, one egg, miso soup, tsukemono, sunomono and Japanese Tea $9.00, 3 Hotcakes 5.50, Papaya 2.00

Lunch:
Daily Specials 11 AM-1:45 PM $11.75 includes rice, miso soup, tsukemono, sunomono and hot green tea: Sakura Tray, Chicken Katsu Teishoku, Teriyaki Chicken, Fish and Vegetable Tempura with Spare Ribs, Chazuke Tray, Pupu Tray, Hamburger Deluxe $5.75, BLT $5.75, Ono Breaded Pork Chops $13.50

Dinner:
Teishoku of miso soup, sashimi, sukiyaki, fried fish, sunomono, tsukemono, rice $13.50. Dinner Combos include rice, miso soup, tsukemono, sunomono and hot green tea: Steak and Shrimp Tempura $20.75, Beef Teriyaki and Shrimp Tempura $17.75, Deep Sea Trio with shrimp tempura, fried fish and sashimi $16.50. Sweet Sour Spare Ribs $11.75, Kona Beef Curry Stew $11.50, New York Steak $14.75, Butterfish $13.50, Juicy Beef Tomato $11.75

Adult Beverages: Beer/Wine/Cocktails

Impressions: Community Center

This family style café and dining room has been a Honalo Town gathering spot for many years. Their reasonably priced menu blends American, Hawaiian, and especially Japanese influences. One dish that successfully combines all three is the Fried Rice with two eggs and ham. This is breakfast and lunch all rolled into one. To accompany the traditional ham and eggs, the fried rice is enhanced with the flavors of green onions, bean sprouts, and sesame oil. If you are traveling to and from the volcano and need a convenient stop for anytime-of-day dining just slide into a booth and experience Teshima's unique style of local comfort food.

Big Island Dining

Kona

Thai Rin ✓✓✓
Alii Sunset Plaza
75-5799 Alii Drive
Kailua-Kona, HI 96740
808-329-2929
Web: None
Hours: LD 11:00 AM-9:00 PM
L Specials 11:00 AM-2:00 PM
Cards: MC V
Dress: Casual
Style: Thai $$

Menu Sampler: Kids Menu Too

Breakfast:
N/A

Lunch/Dinner:
Appetizers: Spring Rolls $5.95, Chicken or Shrimp Satay $7.95/$8.95, Deep Fried Tofu with peanut plum sauce $6.95, Spicy Chicken Wings $8.95
Salads: Green Papaya Salad $5.95, House Salad with peanut sauce $5.95, Combination Seafood Salad with lime-chili dressing $16.95, Chicken or Beef Salad with lime-chili dressing $8.95, House Salad with chicken $8.95
Soups: Lemongrass Soup with Fish $10.95, Noodle Soup with Beef $8.95
Noodles and Rice: Pad Thai with Chicken $9.95, Spicy Noodles with Tofu $9.95, Pineapple Fried Rice with shrimp, cashews and raisins $10.95, Sautéed Rice Noodles with shrimp in soy sauce with eggs, broccoli and cabbage $14.95
Entrées: Chicken with garlic, pepper, broccoli, carrots, cabbage and Thai garlic sauce $9.95, Tofu Stir Fried with bean thread, egg, onion and tomato $9.95, Chicken Panang Curry with peanut sauce, coconut milk, sweet basil and vegetables $9.95, Scallop Macadamia Nuts with onions & vegetables $15.95, Shrimp with special sauce on crispy noodles $15.95, Steamed Mahi $14.95
Special Thai Rin Platter of Fried Spring Rolls, Chicken Satay, Beef Salad, Chicken Wings and Tom Yung Kung - Lemongrass Shrimp Soup $19.95
Desserts: Bananas in Coconut Milk $2.50, Fried Banana $1.95, Ice Cream $2.50
Adult Beverages: Beer/Wine/Cocktails – Corkage Fee $10.00

Impressions: Consistent Quality

Thai Rin is located curbside on Alii Drive and comes complete with sunset and ocean views. Their award-winning menu is a favorite around Kailua-Kona. The prices are reasonable and portions generous. If you are looking for consistently good Thai cuisine in a pleasant, easy to walk to location this place should work.

Big Island Dining

Volcano Village

Thai Thai Restaurant ✓✓✓
19-4084 Old Volcano Road
Volcano, HI 96785
808-967-7969
Web: None
Hours: LD 12:00 PM-8:30 PM Mo-Fr
        D 5:00 PM-8:30 PM SaSu
Cards: AE DIS JCB MC V
Dress: Casual
Style: Thai $$

Menu Sampler: Kids Menu Too

Breakfast/Lunch:
N/A

Dinner:
Appetizers: Spring Rolls of long rice, carrots, cabbage and onion stuffed in a rice-paper wrapper and deep-fried to a golden brown, served with a special sweet and sour sauce $9.99, Chicken or Tofu Satay with special sauce $18.99
Salads: Raw Sliced Green Papaya Salad $9.99, with Jumbo Shrimp or Thai BBQ Chicken with sticky rice or Mixed Seafood $18.99, Chicken Lab $15.99
Soups: Shrimp Thai Ginger Soup made from coconut milk, Thai ginger &lime juice - hot, medium or mild $18.99, Rice Soup w/chicken broth, roasted garlic with shrimp or mahi mahi $18.99, Chicken Lemongrass Spicy & Sour $12.99
Entrées: Shrimp Red Curry with red chili peppers in a curry sauce, coconut milk, Thai eggplant, bamboo and Thai basil $18.99, Chicken Panang Curry with red chili peppers, spices, coconut milk, long beans and seasonal vegetables $12.99, Fresh Eggplant and Thai Basil Stir Fry with special sauce, minced garlic and fresh Thai basil with choice of Chicken, Beef, Pork or Tofu $12.99, Jumbo Shrimp Red Curry with coconut milk $18.99, Chicken Matsaman Curry with potatoes, onions, peanuts $12.99, Ginger Root Stir Fry with Tofu $12.99
Desserts: Thai Tapioca with taro and coconut milk $2.99, Ice Cream $2.99
Adult Beverages: Beer/Wine Cellar/Cocktails – Corkage Fee $20.00

Impressions: Truly Authentic

Nestled in the mists and rain forest on top of Mt. Kilauea travelers will find an unexpected surprise. This attractive Thai restaurant serves an extensive dinner menu and offers proof that a good Asian ethnic meal can be found anywhere in Hawaii. Pay attention to the waiter when he describes the degrees of spiciness. Mainland medium and Thai medium are two completely diverse concepts. The cook won't understand if someone orders their dish seasoned hot and returns it.

Big Island Dining

Kona

The Coffee Shack ✓✓✓
83-5799 Mamalahoa Hwy (Hwy 11)
Captain Cook, HI 96704
808-328-9555
Web: None
Hours: B 7:30 AM-12:00 PM
        L 7:30 AM-3:00 PM
Cards: DIS MC V
Dress: Casual
Style: Coffee House & Deli $

Menu Sampler: Kids Menu Too

Breakfast:
Eggs Benedict with potatoes or rice 10.95, Fresh Fruit Plate 8.95, Three Egg Omelet with Ham, Onion and Cheese, toast, potatoes or rice 9.95, Fried Egg Sandwich with mayo, Swiss cheese, lettuce, tomato 7.95, French Toast 8.95, Great daily special omelettes and benedicts with upscale sauces and fillings
Lunch:
Canadian Bacon BLT 8.95, Black Forest Ham & Smoked Turkey, hot or cold 8.95, Smoked Salmon 9.95, Roast Beef with provolone cheese, lettuce, tomato & mayo 8.95, Hot Corned Beef Reuben with sauerkraut, Swiss cheese, lettuce, Dijon mustard & Russian dressing 8.95, Hot Pastrami with Swiss cheese 8.95
Pizzas: 8" Gourmet Pizzas, Luau Pizza, ham, pineapple, mozzarella & parmesan 11.95, Pepperoni Pizza, mozzarella & parmesan 11.95, Ultimate Meat Pizza, Black Forest Ham, sausage, pepperoni, mozzarella & parmesan cheese 12.95, Gorgonzola Pizza, fresh rosemary, garlic, olive oil, Bermuda onion, mozzarella & parmesan cheese 10.95, Gourmet Veggie Pizza, fresh tomatoes, olives, onions, mushrooms, green pepper, mozzarella, feta & parmesan cheese 11.95
Soups & Salads: Soup of the day $3.95/$5.95, Greek Salad 10.95, Cobb 12.95
Desserts & Pastries: selection may vary daily Carrot Cake 4.95, Lilikoi Cheese Cake 4.95, Assorted Muffins 3.00, Cranberry Scones 2.50, Cinnamon Rolls 4.50
Adult Beverages: Beer/Wine/Champagne

Impressions: Great Kitchen

South of Captain Cook you'll find an unassuming assembly of buildings housing one of the best dining finds we've encountered in years. From the name it would be easy to write it off as just another Kona Coffee parlor. Big mistake! Park your car wherever you can and find a table. Everything served here is top quality and made on premises to the greatest degree possible. Breakfast is a sure-fire winner and lunch follows suit without missing a beat. Save room for homemade dessert!

Kona

The Fish Hopper Seafood and Steaks ✓✓
75-5683 Alii Drive
Kailua-Kona, HI 96740
808-326-2002
www.fishhopper.com/kona
Hours: B 7:30 AM-11:30 AM
           L 11:30 AM-4:00 PM
           D 4:00 PM-9:00 PM
Cards: AE DC DIS JCB MC V
Dress: Casual
Style: Seafood & Steaks $$

Menu Sampler: Kids Menu Too

Breakfast:
Eggs Benedict with potatoes 12.95, Mac Nut Crusted Coconut Brioche French Toast with crème fraiche and berries 11.95, Wild Salmon Omelet 12.95

Lunch:
Appetizers: Coconut Shrimp, sweet chili sauce 10.95, Ahi Sashimi Mkt
Salads: Sesame Crusted Ahi Salad with Coconut Prawns 15.95, Cobb 9.50
Entrées: Grilled Vegetable Panini w/fries 10.95, Fish & Chips with fries 13.95, Panko Crusted Sanddabs w/mashed potatoes in lemon caper herb sauce 13.95, California Crab Alfredo Pasta 14.95, Maple Soy Marinated Skirt Steak 14.95

Dinner:
Appetizers: Clams, Mussels Bordelaise 12.95, Dungeness Crab Cocktail 12.95
Salads: Maui Onion and Tomato Salad 9.95, Classic Caesar Salad 9.50
Entrées: Mahi Mahi Macadamia Nut Crusted with mashed Molokai sweet potatoes, papaya salsa 24.95, Linguine Pasta Isabella 24.95, Broiled Filet of Beef & Lobster Tail, merlot wine sauce with Dungeness Crab mashed potatoes and oyster mushrooms 36.95, 14 oz. Prime Rib, mashed potatoes 27.95
Adult Beverages: Beer/Wine/Cocktails

Impressions: Eco Friendly

Over-harvesting is an international fishing dilemma, and Hawaii is no exception. Read menus around the islands and you'll see the standard mix of ahi, ono, mahi mahi and opakapaka. Enlightened restaurants are trying to address this issue proactively by offering lesser utilized varieties or only those species where numbers are considered safe. That approach is embraced at The Fish Hopper. Their guests will only find unthreatened finfish on the menu. We endorse this effort and since much of what's offered come from shallow coastal waters not often seen around Hawaii, we enjoy the variety. Besides, sanddabs become mighty tasty table fare!

Big Island Dining

Kohala

The Hualalai Grille by Alan Wong √√√√
Four Seasons Resort at Hualalai
100 Ka'upulehu Drive
Kailua-Kona, HI 96740
808-325-8000
www.hualalairesort.com
Hours: D 5:30 PM-9:00 PM XTuWe
Cards: AE DC DIS JCB MC V
Dress: Resort Casual
Style: Hawaii Regional/Pacific Rim $$$

Menu Sampler: Kids Menu Too

Breakfast/Lunch:
N/A
Dinner:
Bar Menu: Grilled Catch Sandwich on an onion bun with caper aioli 17,
Hualalai Grille Burger of grass fed beef, bacon, cheddar cheese, avocado salsa,
crispy onions 17, Local Style Poke 15, Korean Inspired Buffalo Wings with
smoked Big Island goat cheese dressing 18, Chili Cheese Fries of Kona beer
battered sweet potato wedges, ahi chili and spiced aioli 20
Appetizers: Vietnamese Style Pork and Shrimp Spring Rolls with spicy sweet
and sour dipping sauce, butter lettuce wraps 17, Chunky Tartare of spicy ahi
poke, avocado salsa, crispy won ton pi 17, Hoisin Plum BBQ Ribs 18
Salads: Hamakua Springs Salad of greens, tomatoes, Japanese cucumbers,
Ninole hearts of palm, housemade sherry vinaigrette 11, H.R. Caesar Salad with
kalua pig lomi tomato relish 13, Whole Tomato Salad with li hing mui 13
Entrées: Seared Peppered Ahi, crispy Asian slaw, macadamia nuts, soy
vinaigrette 38, Pan Steamed Opakapaka, shrimp and pork hash, truffled nage,
tapioca pearls, gingered vegetables 39, Beef Tenderloin, grilled, roasted
vegetable salad, braised potatoes, Tallicherry pepper foie gras glaze 45, Grilled
Mahi-Mahi with Big Island Pepeaio mushroom and pohole stir fry vegetables,
wasabi butter sauce 37, Grilled Rib Eye Steak, guava smoked chevre gratin 44
Adult Beverages: Beer/Wine Cellar/Cocktails – Corkage Fee 50

Impressions: Elite Clubhouse

The Hualalai Club Grille is what you hope to find when a golf course restaurant
starts taking itself seriously. The end result is more like a private club than part
of a resort hotel. We always liked this room, but you should see it now! One of
Hawaii's premier chefs recently took charge and things went to a new level. All
serious foodies need to put this one on their list. It's definitely worth the effort.

Big Island Dining

Kona

The Royal Thai Café ✓
Keauhou Shopping Center
78-6831 Alii Drive
Kailua-Kona, HI 96740
808-322-8424
Web: None
Hours: L 11:00AM-2:30 PM Mo-Fr
           L 12:00 PM-2:30 PM SaSu
           D 2:30-9:00 PM
Cards: AE DC DIS JCB MC V
Dress: Casual
Style: Thai $$

Menu Sampler:

Breakfast:
N/A

Lunch/Dinner:
Appetizers: Fresh Basil Rolls with shrimp, bean sprouts, basil, green leaf lettuce and plum dipping sauce (not deep fried) $6.95, Chicken Satay with peanut sauce and cucumber salad $7.95, Thai Fried Chicken Wings $8.95
Soup: Chicken Tom Kah Kai, a hot and sour soup with coconut milk, galanga, onion and mushrooms $9.95, Thai Dumpling Soup $9.95, Tofu Soup $9.95
Thai Curries: Beef Green Curry with bamboo shoots, broccoli, cabbage, bell pepper, sweet basil and mushrooms in coconut milk $9.95, Seafood Curry with shrimp, squid, scallops, fillet of fish, red curry in coconut milk $15.95
Specials: Royal Thai Diamond Seafood with broiled lobster tail, giant shrimp, scallops, squid and fillet of fish with mixed vegetables topped with oyster sauce $Mkt, Royal Thai Foursome of shrimp, pork, beef and chicken sautéed with mixed vegetables served on a hot plate $14.95
Noodles & Fried Rice: Combination Fried Rice with chicken, pork and beef pan-fried with rice, egg, onion, tomato and scallions $9.95, Pahd Thai with shrimp, chicken, egg, garnished with peanut and bean sprout $9.95
Adult Beverages: Beer/Wine – Corkage Fee $10.00

Impressions: Good Find

This spacious Thai restaurant is located in the new Keauhou Shopping Center at the south edge of Kona. Forget the mental images of little take-out places before getting in your car because that is not at all the case here. Visitors can expect to find a nicely decorated dining room with a helpful staff serving Thai specialties at mainstream prices. Add it to your list of better tables found around Keauhou.

Big Island Dining

Kohala Coast

The Seafood Bar ✓✓
Kawaihae Harbor
Kawaihae, HI 96743
808-880-9393
www.seafoodbar.com
Hours: L 11:00 AM-2:30 PM
        D 2:30 PM-11:30 PM
Cards: MC V
Dress: Casual
Style: Island $$

Menu Sampler:

Breakfast:
N/A
Lunch:
Salads: Spinach Salad $7, Tofu Sprout Salad with lilikoi dressing $11
Sandwiches: Grilled Fish Plate with fresh catch, rice, vegetables $15, BBQ Pork Hoagie with Asian slaw $9, Seafood Bar Chuck Burger, wasabi mayo, slaw $10, Grilled Fish Wrap with fresh catch $10, Corned Beef Reuben $9
Dinner:
Pupus: Oyster Shooter $2, Ahi Sashimi $Mkt, Escargot with basil pesto butter $10, Pupu Calamari with Furikake, sweet chili tartar sauce $9, Fried Oysters $8
Salads: Greek Tortellini & Shrimp Salad $17, Thai Beef Salad $14, Crab Louis with Alaskan King Crab Meat $17, Greens and Teriyaki Tofu $13
Entrées: Seafood Pizza, shrimp, scallops, fish w/vegetables, black bean sauce on wheat thin crust $17, Ginger Steamed Clams, parmesan cheese bread $18, Poke Burger, seared rare, wasabi mayo, Asian slaw $11, Fried Rice $15, Garlic Ribeye, bleu cheese potatoes, grilled vegetables $28, Shrimp Linguini $25, Southwest Fish & Crab Meat, fresh onion topped w/crab, broiled with pepper-jack cheese, on rice with roasted sweet corn relish and chipotle sour cream $26
Adult Beverages: Beer/Wine/Cocktails

Impressions: Lite Dining

As those who frequent such establishments can attest most bar menus are simple affairs. Once you get past the burger baskets and deep fryer, things tend to wind down pretty quick. Not so at The Seafood Bar. Sure, this is a place where dad's never here and more of the customers have a glass in their hand than a sandwich, but the galley does a respectable job of putting out a variety of light meals. Note that this is a popular gathering spot for the after-work crowd so the kitchen stays open late. That can be a good thing to remember on the quiet side of this island!

Big Island Dining

Kohala Coast

Tommy Bahama's ✓✓✓

The Shops at Mauna Lani
68-1330 Maua Lani Drive
Kohala Coast, HI 96743
808-881-8686
www.tommybahama.com
Hours: D 4:00PM-10:00PM
Cards: AE MC V
Dress: Resort Casual
Style: Island $$$

Menu Sampler: Kids Menu Too

Breakfast/Lunch:
N/A
Dinner:
Appetizers: Crab Calloway, griddled crab cakes with sweet chili mustard sauce and cilantro oil, Asian slaw 19.5, Big Island Goat Cheese with mango salsa 13.5, Loki-Loki Tuna Poke with guacamole, soy and sesame oil, flatbread and tortilla strips 19.5, Coconut Shrimp served with chutney and Asian slaw 19.9
Soups and Salads: Cooper Island Crab Bisque with Tommy's flatbread 9/12, Tommy's Classic Caesar Salad 11, Boca Boca Beet Salad tossed with lilikoi vinaigrette 10, Tortola Tortilla Soup with lime sour cream 6/9
Entrées: Long Island New York Strip with seasoned butter and jumbo onion rings 37, Port-Au-Prince Pork Chop with a port wine demi-glace and grilled pineapple & vegetable skewer 34, Old San Juan Shrimp and Scallops in a coconut curry sauce, rice 34, Tommy's Rib Rack with blackberry brandy barbeque sauce, fries and Asian slaw 37, Sanibel Stuffed Chicken with roasted red pepper cream sauce 31, Opakapaka Haleakala, snapper in a macadamia nut crust, wasabi soy butter sauce, grilled broccolini, lemon garlic oil 38
Adult Beverages: Beer/Wine/Cocktails

Impressions: Island Oasis

Any man, woman, or child who hasn't been to the new Shops at Mauna Lani has an interesting experience in store for them. Imagine several acres of unprotected concrete spread out on a jet black lava field under a cloudless sunny sky and you start to get the picture. It's called, "Man, it's hot outside!" Don't despair because Tommy's retreat is waiting upstairs with cool fans and cold beverages to quench the fire. This concept has worked all over the world and is well represented upon the Kohala Coast. Great preparations are standard fare in this upscale, yet casual bistro. Many of the selections are Caribbean focused creating a change of tastes.

Big Island Dining

Kohala

Tres Hombres Beach Grill ✓✓
Kawaihae Shopping Center
Highway 270
Kawaihae, HI 96743
808-882-1031
Web: None
Hours: LD 11:00 AM-9:00 PM Su-Th
LD 11:00 AM-10:00 PM Fr-Sa
Cards: MC V
Dress: Casual
Style: Mexican $$

Menu Sampler: Kids Menu Too

Breakfast:
N/A
Lunch/Dinner:
Antojitos: Tortilla Chips smothered in chile sauce and refried beans, topped with jack cheese, fresh tomatoes, green onions and jalapenos garnished with sour cream and guacamole $7.95/$10.95/$13.95, Plato Grande of taquitos, guacamole, quesadillas, calamari and nachos serving 4 or more $22.95
Soups & Salads: Island Salad of greens topped with sliced avocado, onion, tomato and fresh papaya $10.95, with chicken breast $12.95, steak $15.95, or Mahi Mahi $18.95, Soup of the Day $4.95, Mexican Salad w/veggies $11.95
The Beach Grill: Two Chicken Breasts with a honey mustard glaze $16.95, Large Pacific Shrimp basted in lime and cilantro butter $17.95, Full Rack of Baby Back Ribs with refried beans, small salad and a cheese quesadilla $22.95
Combinaciones: all served with refried beans and Spanish rice, Enchilada, Taco, Tostada, or Chile Relleno, one choice $9.95, two $12.95, three $16.95
Comidas Especiales: all served with refried beans and Spanish rice, Crab Enchilada with pepper cheese, topped with green sauce, guacamole and sour cream $19.95, Two Carne Asada Tacos w/grilled seasoned steak in soft flour tortillas with cheese and pico de gallo and guacamole $16.95, Chile Poblano stuffed with crab, shrimp and jack cheese, battered and baked, topped with tomatillo cream sauce and sour cream $20.95, Two Shrimp Tacos $17.95
A la Carte: Beef or Chicken Taco $4.95, Fish Taco $6.95, Shrimp Taco $8.95
Adult Beverages: Beer/Wine/Cocktails

Impressions: Surfer Tex/Mex

Welcome to Baja on the Big Island! This second floor ocean view cantina is a welcome find on the parched North Kohala Coast. Margaritas! Tacos! Andale!

Kona

U-top-it ✓✓
Alii Sunset Plaza
75-5799 Alii Drive
Kailua-Kona, HI 96740
808-329-0092
Web: None
Hours: BL 7:00 AM-2:00 PM XMo
Cards: AE DC DIS JCB MC V
Dress: Casual
Style: Island $

Menu Sampler: Kids Menu Too

Breakfast:
Hawaiian Taro PanCrepes, plain 3.95, topped with a variety of meats, cheeses, fruits and vegetables for .50/1.00 each, Grilled Veggie PanCrepe with curry or hollandaise sauce 8.95, Kanak Attack with Portuguese Sausage, Spam & onions in a PanCrepe topped with fried rice & two eggs 6.95, Hula Girl Sweet Stack with three PanCrepes, vanilla cream, mac nuts & bananas 6.95, Breakfast Combo with two eggs any style, choice of meat and choice of starch with country gravy or a PanCrepe with one topping 7.25, Cheese Quesadilla 5.95

Lunch:
1/2# Cheeseburger, fries 8.95, Chicken Curry Breast with rice and choice of vegetables 9.95, Teriyaki Beef with special sweet ginger shoyu sauce 9.95, Rancher's Hoedown of chopped steak and onions with rice or potatoes 8.95, Crispy Grilled Pork Chops w/salad and rice or potatoes 10.95, Seafood Catch of grilled shrimp, scallops, brochette w/tangy garlic sauce, angel hair pasta 13.95

Adult Beverages: Beer/Wine

Dinner:
N/A

Impressions: Innovative Cafe

Breakfast and lunch joints can be a bit predictable. That's good because early in the day people tend to stick with familiar choices. Well, tell the scrambled eggs to move over because café dining just took a turn up the high road. Welcome to the house of taro crepes where no topping is too daring. Think of taking the guy who invented the Denver Omelette and pairing him with a Hawaiian Local Boy and you get the mindset in this kitchen. It all seems to work out with sweet and savory island kine dishes served side-by-side to happy customers all around. Of course, there's also lunch when those favoring local food get their turn to grind. You don't have to march to the beat of a different drum to enjoy this new place.

Big Island Dining

Kona

Wasabi's Japanese Cuisine ✓
Coconut Grove Marketplace
75-5803 Alii Drive
Kailua-Kona, HI 96740
808-326-2352
www.wasabishawaii.com
Hours: L 11:00 AM-3:00 PM
          D 3:00 PM-10:00 PM
Cards: JCB MC V
Dress: Casual
Style: Japanese $$

Menu Sampler: Kids Menu Too

Breakfast:
N/A
Lunch:
Teri Chicken and Rice Bowl $5.95, Katsu Chicken and Rice Bowl $8.50, Yakisoba $8.50, Spicy Chow Funn Noodles, chef's special $8.50, Special Combo, Teri Chicken, 4 pc California Roll, salad, rice $8.50, Bentos $8/$12, Sushi Plates, 9 pc $14.95 to 15 pc $18.95, Tempura Udon $9.50
Dinner:
Entrées: Tempura & Teri Chicken $12.95, Katsu Combo $12.95, Steak, Tempura and Teri Salmon $18.95, Beef Shabu Shabu for Two $39.95, Steak and Tempura $16.95, Unagi w/soup, salad & rice $16.95, Sukiyaki for Two $39.95
Sushi Plates: Oahu, 5 pcs of nigiri & 10 pcs of rolled sushi $18.95, Alii Feast, 4 pcs Nigiri sushi, 8 pcs deluxe California roll & 2 hand rolled $21.95
Sushi: California Roll or Avocado Roll $6.50, Hamachi Roll $7.50, Fresh Dungeness Crab Roll $10.50, Tempura Shrimp Roll $10.00, Crazy Roll of tempura shrimp roll covered with spicy ahi sashimi-crispy $16.00, A Ling's Special Roll, California Roll covered with Unagi & special sauce $15.00, Tempura Veggie Roll $7.00, Salmon Skin Roll $7.50, Ume Roll $6.00
Adult Beverages: Beer/Wine

Impressions: Simple Pleasure

Things have changed lately at Wasabi's Japanese Cuisine. The owners recently expanded this busy sushi shop into the world of full service dining. Guests will find a considerably more ambitious menu complete with nabemono dishes like sukiyaki and shabu shabu. Of course the sushi and sashimi specialties continue to be offered. Look for this establishment in a building shared with the kava bar. You'll find plenty of free parking in the shopping center lot behind the complex.

BIG ISLAND OF HAWAII
DINING BY REGION

Big Island Of Hawaii Dining By Region

Kohala

Kona

Volcano Village

Hilo

Waimea

HAWAII
FOOD & CULTURE
GLOSSARY

Hawaii Food & Culture Glossary

a'a	rough clinker lava
aina	the land
abalone	large saltwater mollusk
aburage	deep-fried tofu
adobo	marinated Filipino chicken and/or pork stew
agemono	Japanese cooking method of preparing meats and vegetables by deep-frying
ahi	yellowfin tuna, often served raw as sashimi on a bed of Chinese cabbage with a wasabi and shoyu dipping sauce
ahupua'a	a land division used in old Hawaii consisting of all the lands between two adjoining ridges from the top of the mountain to the ocean
akamai	clever or smart
akua	spirit or god
ali'i	chief or noble
aloha	versatile term that can mean hello, good-bye, and love
Aloha Friday	casual dress day or more importantly the first day of the weekend party that actually starts Thursday afternoon
arroz	rice
arugula	peppery flavored greens
aumakua	guardian spirit
auntie	any older lady, a term of respect

'awa	kava, a beverage made from the ground roots of the intoxicating pepper
azuki	red beans
banh hoi	Vietnamese meat and vegetable roll-up
barbecue stick	char grilled teriyaki meat stick
bean curd	tofu
bean threads	fine thin noodles made from mung bean starch, long rice
bento	Japanese box lunch
black beans	fermented beans used in Chinese sauces
bok choy	a tall variety of cabbage with white celery like stems and dark green leaves
bulgoki	Korean teriyaki barbecue beef
bun	thin soft Vietnamese rice noodles
butterfish	black cod, has a smooth silky texture
carne	meat
cascaron	Filipino fried sweet dumpling
char siu	sweet marinated barbecued pork
chili oil	liquid fire made from chili peppers and oil
Chinese cabbage	a compact variety of cabbage with white celery-like stems and pale green leaves, also known as Napa cabbage or won bok
chorizo	hot and spicy sausage
chow	stir-fry
chow fun	cooked noodles combined with green onions and bits of meat or seafood then stir-fried with sesame oil

chun	Korean method of frying using flour followed by an egg wash
cilantro	Chinese parsley
coconut creme	thick creamy layer on top of a can of coconut milk
coconut milk	liquid extracted by squeezing grated coconut meat
crack seed	sweet or sour snack foods made from preserved fruits and seeds
da kine	what-cha-ma-call-it
daikon	large white Asian root vegetable commonly used as a garnish
dashi	broth made from dried seaweed and flakes of dried bonito
Diamond Head	directional term used on Oahu meaning to go east in the direction of Diamond Head or "Go Diamond Head"
dim sum	Chinese style dumplings
doce	sweet
donburi	thinly sliced meat, vegetables, and coddled egg served in a deep bowl over rice
edamame	lightly salted and boiled young soybeans
egg roll	fried pastry roll with various meat and vegetable fillings
Ewa	directional term used on Oahu meaning to go west in the direction of Ewa or "Go Ewa" which is opposite from Diamond Head and toward Pearl Harbor
fish cake	ground white fish, starch, and salt cooked together by steaming or frying
fish sauce	potent seasoning made from salt and fish

five spice powder	mixture of several spices that usually includes fennel, peppercorns, cinnamon, cloves, and star anise.
furikake	a dry condiment used on rice dishes
fusion cuisine	layers of flavor, texture, temperatures, and techniques created by combining elements from the cuisines of different cultures
ginger	spicy pungent root vegetable used as a flavoring in Asian cooking
gobo	burdock root
grinds	food
guava	sweet red tropical fruit
guisates	Filipino pork or chicken dish made with peas and pimento in a tomato based sauce
hale	house or building
halo halo	tropical fruit sundae made with ice, milk and sugar instead of ice cream, to mix - mix
ham har	fermented dried shrimp paste, very funky, a little goes a long way
hana	work
hana hou	do it one more time/encore!
haole	Caucasian
hapa	half as in hapa-haole or half-Caucasian
haupia	coconut custard dessert
Hawaii Regional Cuisine	movement started in the late '80's/early '90's by young local chefs combining island cooking styles and classic techniques with fresh local products to create an exciting new fusion cuisine

Hawaiian chili water	liquid heat made with Hawaiian chili peppers, water, and salt
Hawaiian rock salt	coarse white or pink rock salt
Hawaiian time	later rather than sooner
heiau	ancient Hawaiian stone temple
hekka	a stir-fry dish made with meat and vegetables in a shoyu-based sauce
hibachi	small charcoal cooker
hoisin sauce	thick, sweet, but pungent sauce used in Chinese cooking
holoholo	pleasure trip, to go "holoholo"
hono	bay
honu	turtle
hukilau	pulling of a large fish net by a group
hui	club or association
hula	Hawaiian native dance
huli huli	"turn turn" as in grilling chicken
imu	Hawaiian underground oven made by digging a pit and lining it with hot lava rocks covered by banana plants and food and burying it for several hours, used at luaus for making kalua pork, laulau, sweet potatoes, etc.
inari sushi	cone sushi made by filling fried tofu pockets with sweet vinegar flavored rice
ipo	sweetheart
kaffir lime leaves	leaves of the kaffir lime tree used as flavoring in Thai cooking

kahuna	priest or skilled person
kai	the sea
kaiseki	Japanese fine dining in courses
kal bi ribs	Korean teriyaki beef short ribs
kale	Portuguese cabbage
kalo	taro
kalua pork	shredded pork prepared luau style in an imu pit, also known locally as kalua pig
kama'aina	long time resident or someone who was born in Hawaii
kamaboko	Japanese fish cake
kane	man
kapu	forbidden
kapuna	grandparent or wise older person
katsu	breaded cutlet
kau kau	food, a place to eat
keiki	child
kiawe	dry land hardwood used in smoking and grilling meats
ki'i	statue or image
kim chee	spicy Korean condiment made from fermented cabbage and peppers
koa	valuable hardwood tree, warrior
Koko Head	directional term used on Oahu meaning to go in the direction of Koko Head or "Go Koko Head"
kokua	help

kona	leeward
kona wind	muggy airflow from the equator
kukui	candlenut tree, the source of kukui nut oil
Kula	a truck gardening district in Upcountry Maui
kulolo	sweet pudding made with poi
kumu	teacher as in kumu hula
lanai	deck or patio
lau hala	woven mats
lau lau	flavored meat mixed with taro leaves and wrapped in ti leaves then steamed, often in an imu
laver	purple seaweed used in making nori
lechon	roasted pig
lei	garland of flowers
lemon grass	woody lemon flavored grass used as flavoring in Southeast Asian cooking
li hing mui	sweet and sour seasoning made from dried plums and salt
lilikoi	passion fruit
limu	edible seaweed
linguica	spicy Portuguese pork sausage seasoned with garlic and paprika
loa	long
loco moco	local dish consisting of rice, a large hamburger patty or slices of Spam, and fried eggs with lots of brown gravy over all
lolo	crazy

lomi	to knead or massage
lomi lomi salmon	salted salmon finely diced with tomatoes and green onions
long rice	clear noodles cooked in broth
lua	restroom
luau	Hawaiian feast, also a dish made from taro leaves, coconut crème, and meat
lulu	calm
lumpia	fried spring roll with meat, vegetable, or dessert fillings
lup cheong	Chinese pork sausage
lychee	sweet white fruit
macadamia nuts	small round nut with creamy but crunchy texture
mac salad	macaroni and mayonnaise
mahalo	thank you
mainland	North America
makai	directional term that is helpful on an island meaning to turn or look toward the ocean
maki sushi	sushi rolled in nori
malasada	wonderful sweet brought here by the Portuguese similar to a fresh sugar donut but minus the hole
malihini	newcomer
malo	loincloth
mana	power or energy from the spirit world
manapua	steamed pork bun

mandoo	Korean dumplings with meat and vegetable fillings
mango	golden fleshed tropical fruit
mano	shark
Manoa	a gardening district near Honolulu, the Manoa Valley
mauka	directional term meaning to look or turn toward the mountain or uphill part of an island
mauna	mountain
mein	Chinese noodles
mele	chant or song
menehune	legendary "little people" of Hawaii
mirin	sweet rice cooking wine
miso	fermented soybean paste
miso soup	light Japanese soup made from soybean paste and garnished with tofu, kamaboko, daikon, green onions, and wakame
mixed plate	plate lunch version of a mixed grill
moa	native Polynesian chicken
moana	ocean
mochi	rice cake
mochiko	sweet rice flour
mo'o	lizard or water spirit
musubi	rice ball
muu muu	loose fitting ankle length dress

naan	Indian flatbread
nabemono	Japanese cooking method of preparing thin slices of meat and vegetables in a hot broth
'Nalo	As in Waimanalo, a garden district on the Windward side of Oahu
nam pla	Thai fish sauce
nam prik	Thai hot sauce
nani	beautiful
nene	Hawaiian goose
nigiri sushi	oblong sushi
niu	coconut
noni	native shrub bearing medicinal fruit
nori	roasted seaweed pressed into sheets
norimaki	sushi rolled in nori
nui	big or great
nuoc mam	Vietnamese fish sauce
off-island	in the islands one does not go "out of town" they go "off-island"
ogo	type of seaweed favored by the Japanese
ohana	extended family
ohelo	native shrub bearing edible berries
okazuya	a Japanese delicatessen where fast foods and snacks are served buffet style
ono	delicious
opae	shrimp

opihi	Hawaiian escargot harvested from rocks along the ocean and eaten raw with salt
oyster sauce	thick brown sauce made from oysters and shoyu often used in stir fry dishes
Pacific Rim Cuisine	a fusion of cuisines involving methods and ingredients from the countries around the Pacific Ocean
pad thai	Thai noodles
pahoehoe	smooth ropey lava
pakalolo	crazy smoke, marijuana, buds; something to decline when offered
pali	cliff
pancit	Filipino noodles
paniolo	Hawaiian cowboy
panko	Japanese breadcrumbs
pao	bread
pao doce	Portuguese sweet bread
papaya	smooth skinned orange-fleshed tropical fruit that can also be used green when peeled and shredded in a salad
pasteles	similar to a tamale except made with bananas instead of corn flour
patis	Filipino fish sauce
pau	finished
pau hana	finished working
pho	Vietnamese noodle soup
pidgin	Hawaiian Creole English
pipi kaula	Hawaiian beef jerky

plantain	cooking banana
plate lunch	island style blue plate special with a main entrée such as teriyaki beef or chicken, two scoops of white rice, and a scoop of macaroni salad
poi	glutinous paste made by pounding steamed taro root, the Hawaiian staple starch
poke	ceviche dish made with cubed fish or sliced octopus mixed with onion and seaweed then marinated in shoyu and spices
pono	righteous
ponzu	tart Japanese citrus sauce
Portuguese sausage	spicy garlic and paprika flavored pork sausage, linguica
pua	flower
pua'a	pig
pueo	owl
puka	hole
pupu	appetizer
pu'u	hill
ramen	curly Japanese wheat noodles
rice noodle	noodles made with rice flour
rice paper	round rice flour wrapper that is soaked in hot water to soften before use
saimin	island noodle soup that has many variations and broths--extras may include Spam, teriyaki beef, green onions, vegetables, hard-cooked eggs, and fish cake

sake	Japanese rice wine
sashimi	raw fish sliced very thin and served with spicy condiments and dipping sauce
satay	tender chicken or beef strips marinated in coconut milk and spices then skewered and grilled
sesame oil	aromatic oil made from sesame seeds used sparingly to flavor Asian dishes
shabu shabu	chafing dish cookery involving thinly sliced meats and vegetables simmered in broth usually with a tabletop preparation
shaka	hand signal using the thumb and little finger used as a greeting
shave ice	similar to a snow cone except there is no crunch as the ice is shaved instead of crushed, can be topped with wonderful tropical flavored syrups and served with ice cream and azuki beans
shoyu	Japanese soy sauce, Aloha Brand is preferred in the islands as it is not as salty as some other types
soba	Japanese buckwheat noodles
somen	thin Japanese wheat noodles
Spam	canned spiced pork lunchmeat
spring roll	fried rice paper roll with various fillings
starch	rice or potatoes
sukiyaki	Japanese beef, tofu, vegetable, and noodle dish with shoyu based sauce commonly cooked at the table
summer roll	fresh rice paper roll with various fillings
sushi	small slices of vegetables, fruits, fish, or meat combined with tangy rice

sweet bread	rich egg bread commonly called Molokai or Portuguese sweet bread
sweet rice	also known as sticky rice or glutinous rice
tako	octopus
talk story	to have a casual conversation
tapa	cloth made from pounded tree bark
taro	starchy root plant used in making poi
teri	teriyaki
teishoku	a complete Japanese meal including soup, salad, entrée, pickled vegetables, and rice
tempura	meat, seafood, or vegetables fried in a light batter coating
tendon	meat and vegetable tempura served over rice
teppanyaki	Japanese cooking method of grilling vegetables, seafood, meat and rice tableside by a knife-wielding chef, very entertaining
teriyaki	sweet tangy shoyu based marinade
Thai basil	herb used in Thai cooking, has a purple flower and sharper taste than sweet basil
ti	broad-leafed plant whose leaves are used for plates, hula skirts, and for wrapping foods and religious offerings
tobiko	flying fish roe, caviar
tofu	soybean curd available fresh or fermented
tom yum	spicy Thai soup
tonkatsu	fried cutlet
tsukemono	pickled vegetables

tuong ot	Vietnamese hot sauce
tutu	grandmother
two scoop rice	two scoops of cooked white rice
uala	sweet potato
udon	thick Japanese wheat noodles
ulu	breadfruit
vertical food	a physical manifestation of fusion cuisine where the elements of the dish are stacked
wahine	woman
wai	water
wakame	a seaweed condiment
wasabi	spicy Japanese horseradish paste often combined sparingly with shoyu to make a dipping sauce for sushi and sashimi
wiki wiki	hurry up, very fast
wok	round bottomed cooking pot used over very high heat to quick sear or stir-fry chopped meats and vegetables
won bok	Chinese cabbage
won ton	Chinese meat dumplings
wor	vegetables
yakimono	Japanese cooking method of preparing meats and vegetables by broiling or grilling
yakiniku	tabletop grilling
yakisoba	grilled noodles
yakitori	grilled meat and vegetable kebabs

HAWAII
FISH & SEAFOOD
GLOSSARY

`Hawaii Fish & Seafood Glossary

Hawaii IS the island state, and what could be a more fitting centerpiece on a Hawaiian menu than the bounty of the sea? Just like everything else found in this Pacific paradise there are unique spins to the fish and seafood selections. With this in mind we have created a separate glossary to help you explore and better appreciate the aquatic offerings found in Hawaii's dining spots.

Visitors need to be aware that finfish are nearly always listed by their Hawaiian names on island menus. That's no problem for those who grew up in Hawaii, but the rest of us would do well to brush up on the subject first. How else would you know that an ahi is a big eye or yellow fin tuna, and that a tako is definitely not the same as a taco? The word tako in Hawaii means octopus and receiving one instead of the other could come as quite a surprise!

Most people don't realize that longliners stay out for several days at a time, but trollers come in every night and that the difference in the quality and freshness of their catch can be noticed. If you are paying for fresh island fish you want to make sure that you get it. You might see the term day boat used in some of the finer restaurants to describe the freshest of fresh fish and seafood. Regardless, make sure to ask and always insist on fish that has never been frozen.

As long as we're on the subject of getting what you're paying for, let's take a look at the economics of fish and seafood in Hawaii. There's a misconception that just because people see "water, water everywhere", the aquatic resources must be limitless and their prices low. Nothing could be farther from the truth. The high cost of production through aquaculture and harvest in the wild along with huge local and foreign demand drive prices to the upper limit of the menu.

In closing, when you decide to take the plunge and go out for fish or seafood, make it a point to trust the recommendations at the restaurant. The chef knows how to match species and preparations for the best possible results. Just let your waiter know what you have in mind and listen to his suggestions. You'll be far happier in the end if you go with the flow than if you try to have it your way.

ahi	big eye or yellow fin tuna
aku	skipjack tuna, most common spring through early fall, robust flavor, firm texture, often served as poke or in sushi, primarily caught by commercial pole-and-line fishermen and recreational trollers
akule	big-eyed scad, a local favorite, primarily caught by netting or by hook-and-line fishermen

ama ebi	sweet shrimp or langoustines, harvested with traps from deep water, available locally but often imported
a'u	billfish of any type
big eye ahi	big eye tuna, most common from mid-fall through mid-spring, moderate beef-like flavor, medium firm texture, favored for sashimi and poke, primarily caught by long-line boats
ehu	red snapper, moderate flavor, most common during winter, medium firm texture, primarily caught by deepwater hook-and-line fishermen
hapu'upu'u	grouper or sea bass, most common spring and fall, moderate flavor, medium firm texture, primarily caught by deepwater hook-and-line fishermen
hebi	shortbill spearfish, most common mid-spring through early fall, moderate flavor, medium firm texture, primarily caught by commercial long-line boats
kajiki	pacific blue marlin, most common summer through fall, moderate flavor, firm texture, primarily caught by commercial long-line boats and recreational trollers
Keahole lobster	clawed "Maine" lobsters raised on the Big Island through aquaculture, available all year
Kona lobster	spiny or rock lobster, primarily caught by divers working the reef or by trapping, usually imported, available all year
lehi	silver mouth snapper, most common during late fall and winter, moderate flavor, medium texture, primarily caught by deepwater hook-and-line fishermen

mahimahi	dolphinfish, most common spring and fall, moderate almost sweet flavor, medium texture, ask if the fish is fresh "island fish", primarily caught by commercial and recreational trollers
moi	pacific threadfin, the royal fish, now raised locally through aquaculture, mild flavor, delicate texture, available all year
monchong	bigscale or sickle pomfret, available all year, robust flavor, medium firm texture, primarily caught as a by-catch of tuna long-liners and deepwater hook-and-line fishermen.
nairagi	striped marlin, most common winter and spring, moderate flavor, medium firm texture, primarily caught by commercial long-line boats and recreational trollers
onaga	ruby or long-tailed red snapper, most common late fall and winter, mild flavor, medium texture, primarily caught by deepwater hook-and-line fishermen
ono	wahoo, most common late spring through early fall, mild almost citrus-like flavor, medium firm texture, primarily caught by commercial and recreational trollers with part of the catch harvested by commercial long-line fishermen
opae	shrimp, now raised locally through aquaculture, available all year
opah	moonfish, most common spring through summer, robust flavor, medium texture, primarily caught by commercial long-line fishermen fishing over seamounts
opakapaka	crimson snapper, most common fall and winter, mild flavor, delicate texture, primarily caught by deepwater hook-and-line fishermen

opihi	small limpet, found on coastal rock faces in the surf zone, eaten raw with salt as "Hawaiian escargot"
papio	juvenile pompano or crevally, medium flavor, firm texture, caught by shore casters, shallow water trollers, and bottom fishermen
shutome	broadbill swordfish, most common spring and summer, moderate flavor, medium firm texture, caught at night by commercial long-line fishermen
tako	octopus or squid, primarily caught by divers working in shallow water or by jigging
tombo	albacore or "white meat" tuna, most common mid-spring through mid-fall, moderate flavor, medium texture, primarily caught by commercial long-line fishermen and small-boat hand line fishermen
uku	grey snapper, most common mid-spring through mid-fall, moderate flavor, medium firm texture, primarily caught in deep water by hook-and-line fishermen but is also caught near the surface by recreational trollers
ula	spiny or rock lobster, primarily caught by divers working the reef or by trapping
ula papapa	slipper lobster, primarily caught by divers working the reef or by trapping
ulua	adult pompano or crevally, medium flavor, firm texture, caught by shore casters, shallow water trollers, and bottom fishermen
yellow fin ahi	yellow fin tuna, most common mid-spring through mid-fall, moderate beef-like flavor, medium firm texture, favored for sashimi and poke, primarily caught by commercial long-line boats and commercial and recreational trollers

Hawaii Restaurant Guide Series

Kauai Restaurants And Dining
With Princeville And Poipu Beach
ISBN 1-931752-37-0 $8.95 US

Maui Restaurants And Dining
With Lanai And Molokai
ISBN 1-931752-38-9 $9.95 US

Oahu Restaurants And Dining
With Honolulu And Waikiki
ISBN 1-931752-39-7 $9.95 US

Big Island Of Hawaii Restaurants And Dining
With Hilo And The Kona Coast
ISBN 1-931752-40-0 $8.95 US

Hawaii Budget Restaurants And Dining
With All Six Hawaiian Islands
ISBN 1-931752-41-9 $8.95 US

Individual Orders Can Be Placed Through All Major
Book Retailers. Inquiries On Wholesale Or Quantity
Orders Can Be Sent To The Ingram Book Company

- Or -

Holiday Publishing Inc
PO Box 11120
Lahaina, HI 96761

holidaypublishing@yahoo.com
www.hawaiirestaurantguide.com

BIG ISLAND GRILL .GOOD

FISH & HOG - WAIMEA !
              - VERY GOOD. !

CPSIA information can be obtained at www.ICGtesting.com
Printed in the USA
240771LV00003B/55/P